Sailing's a Breeze!
with 153 visual aids

Aquatics Unlimited, Inc.
Boston, MA

Written by Mark B. Solomon.

Edited by Gary B. Solomon.

Black & white photography by Robert Tannenbaum.

Color photography by Amy L. Solomon.

Graphic artwork by Mark B. Solomon.

Shot on location at Camp Avoda, Middleboro, MA.

Published by Aquatics Unlimited, Inc., Boston, MA.

Distributed by: ICS Books, Inc, 1370 E. 86th Place, Merrillville, IN 46410 (800) 541-7323

Preface

The four sections of *Sailing's a Breeze!* are individual learning units. The student learns a complete skill set in each section: sailing knowledge tools, sailing theory, practical skills, and knots for sailors. Each section builds upon the skills taught in the previous section. The review questions and answers allow the student to measure his or her learning progress.

Crew Section:
The Crew section is designed to educate the student in sailing fundamentals. At the end of the Crew section, the student should be able to aid more experienced sailors and actually control the helm.

2nd Mate Section:
The 2nd Mate section is designed to educate the student in practical sailing issues. At the end of the 2nd Mate section, the student, under supervision, should be able to control the helm throughout all phases of a normal sailing day.

1st Mate Section:
The 1st Mate section is designed to educate the student in more advanced practical skills. At the end of the 1st Mate section, the student should be able to captain a sailboat with the aid of a crew.

Captain Section:
The Captain section is designed to educate the student in advanced sailing theory. At the end of the Captain section, the student should be able to sail solo and to handle the craft proficiently.

We dedicate this book to our parents, Barbara and Leonard Solomon, for providing us the opportunity to spend our childhood years at summer camp, for being our education role models, and for being so supportive throughout the entire *"Sailing's a Breeze!"* project.

Table of Contents

Table of Contents

Table of Contents

Captain Practical 87
- Solo sailing
- Beaching

Captain Knots 89
- Eye splice
- Whipping
- Making a mooring
- Monkey's fist

Aquatics Unlimited presents <u>Sailing's a Breeze!</u> and your sailing instructors, Gary and Mark.

Welcome aboard! Today we'll be learning the finer points of sailing: everything from sailboat nomenclature and marlinspike seamanship to goosewing jibes and sailboat propulsion theories.

Figure 1. Your sailing instructors, Mark and Gary

That's right, Mark. This will be an exciting day on the water, as always. We'll be covering all that you just mentioned and much more in our outdoor classroom. Don't worry if Mark's words sounded foreign; *by the end of this course, we'll all be speaking the same language.*

Figure 2. Hiking out

Introduction

- Safety
- Required equipment
- Use of PFD

Safety is just another word for common sense, and in sailing, like all watersports, one must *always be prepared for the unexpected.*

Figure 3. Unexpected event

When putting on a Type II **PFD** (Personal Flotation Device), we *listen* for the click, *adjust* the fit, and *tie* the top in a bow.

Figure 4. Listen for the click and adjust the fit

Always be sure that you are wearing a PFD correctly rated for your weight. This information can be found on the Coast Guard approval label located on the rear of the PFD.

Figure 5. Secure the PFD

The difference between Lara's **Type II PFD** and Gary's **Type III PFD** is head support. The Type II PFD is designed to keep the wearer's breathing passages clear of the water if the wearer should become unconscious.

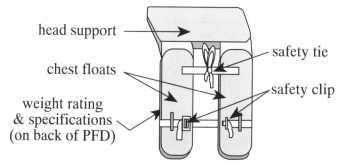

head support

chest floats

weight rating & specifications (on back of PFD)

safety tie

safety clip

Figure 6. Type II PFD

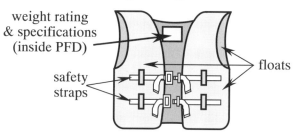

weight rating & specifications (inside PFD)

safety straps

floats

Figure 7. Type III PFD

Experienced sailors often wear a Type III PFD because it provides more movement freedom than the Type II PFD. The decision to use a Type III PFD or a Type II PFD should be based on the user's boating experience, swimming ability, and weather and water conditions.

Maintain the PFD's safety qualities by hanging it to *dry*, keeping it *clean*, and especially *not* using it as a seat cushion. Be good to your PFD; *it may just save your life.*

Figure 8. Unconscious victim

Wearing **shoes** with non-skid soles protects feet from injury and reduces the likelihood of slipping on wet surfaces. A high numbered **sunscreen** correct for your skin type should be applied before sailing.

Figure 9. Wear shoes   *Figure 10. Wear sunscreen*

Wearing sunglasses with UV protection is a must to protect the eyes.

Figure 11. Wear sunglasses

Wearing **appropriate clothing** will make our boating experience more comfortable, but good judgement in this regard also protects us from medical conditions, such as sunstroke, heat exhaustion, and hypothermia. For example, wool is a good fabric to wear when sailing in cold weather because it provides warmth and dries from the inside. We recommend seeking current medical literature on the dangers which can result from prolonged exposure to the elements.

Figure 12. Wear clothing appropriate for the weather conditions

The **required and recommended safety equipment** is as important as proper protection from the elements. Prepared sailors always have audible and visual **distress signals** available on the craft and are informed of current Coast Guard regulations.

Figure 13. Audible, visual signals

A sailboat has many moving parts that wear over time, and a sailboat always has potential for capsizing. These two factors are enough to suggest that we should bring along additional safety items to allow for a self-rescue. Some items to include are: **a bailer, spare PFD, extra line, heaving line, paddle,** and **anchor.**

Figure 14. Some recommended safety equipment

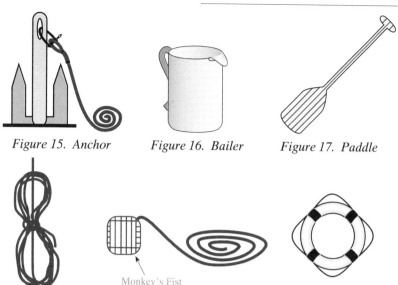

Figure 15. Anchor   Figure 16. Bailer   Figure 17. Paddle

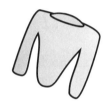

Monkey's Fist

Figure 18. Extra Line   Figure 19. Heaving Line   Figure 20. Ring Buoy

Figure 21. Warm Weather Shirt   Figure 22. Cold Weather Sweater

Figure 23. Whistle   Figure 24. Visual Distress Signal

Common sense suggests knowing your limits. *Recognize your abilities, be aware* of other craft, shallow water, rocks, and other obstructions. Always inform someone on shore that you are on the water, and be sure to have **proper supervision**. And, in case of an emergency, be prepared to use the audible and visual distress signals.

15

Crew Tools

- Nomenclature
- Boarding operations
- Rigging & derigging
- Securing the boat after use

Tools are important for getting a job done. As sailing Crew members, we should have some basic *knowledge tools* at our disposal to communicate with other sailors. Boat **nomenclature** (names of parts of the boat) is a sailor's most important communication tool. Let's review some sailboat nomenclature basics...

The captain faces the **bow**, or front of the boat, and is seated in the rear of the boat, called the **stern**. The **port** is the side on captain's left - note four letters in *port* and *left* - and the **starboard** is the side to captain's right. The **mast** is the pole pointing to the sky, and the **boom** is the horizontal pole that swings across the **deck** low enough to make a *boom* sound when hitting a sailor's head.

The **tiller**, connected to the **rudder**, is the sailboat's steering wheel. The tiller and rudder are attached to the rear, vertical wall of the **hull**, referred to as the **transom**. The top of the sides is known as the **gunwales**. The **centerboard**, or **daggerboard** if removable, is the vertical piece extending beneath the boat. On large boats, the fixed centerboards are referred to as **keels**. The **centerboard cabin** houses the centerboard when the boat is moored. Two lines we need to know are the **halyards**, which are used to hoist sails (*halyards hoist*), and **sheets**, which are used to control sails while sailing underway.

The two types of boats we will be using are called a sloop rig and a lateen rig. A **sloop rig** craft is equipped with two sails - a mainsail and a jib sail. A **lateen rig** is a single sail craft. There are many different types of sailboats; however, since sloop and lateen rigs are very common types of sailboats on which people learn to sail, we will be using sloop and lateen rig craft during our lessons.

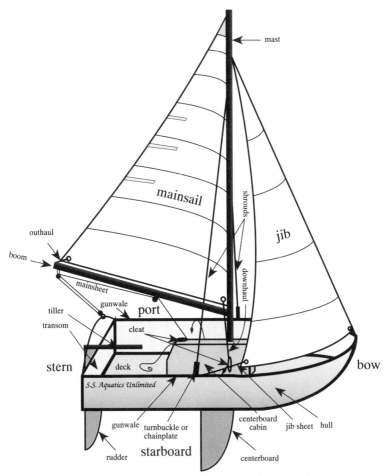

Figure 25. Sailboat nomenclature (sloop rig)

Figure 26. Sloop and lateen rig sailboats

The *intangible nomenclature* we should know at this point includes the **windward side** and the **leeward side**. The windward side is the side of the boat the wind strikes first; the leeward side is simply the other side. For example, if the wind is striking the port side, port is said to be the windward side.

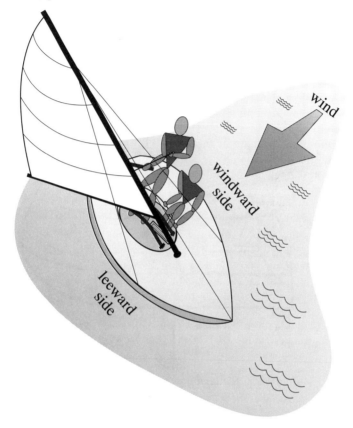

Figure 27. Intangible nomenclature: windward and leeward side

When **boarding and deboarding** any craft, we "shift our weight" as we step behind our hands. Notice that Lara holds onto both the point of entry and exit to keep her body low. Keeping low improves her balance on the boat and the boat's balance on the water. Plugs for through-transom drains, if the boat is so equipped, are inserted, and the centerboard or daggerboard is lowered. Finally, gear is transferred and stowed to make room for other crew. During and after boarding, we place our gear and ourselves about the craft such that the sailboat remains balanced.

Figure 28. Shift weight while boarding

Preparing the craft for sailing is known as **rigging**. Before we begin the rigging process, it is important to note that the sailboat's bow should remain pointing into the wind and that the boom and sails be free to move in the direction of the wind during the entire rigging process. By keeping the craft pointing into the wind while rigging and allowing the sails to move freely without catching wind, sailors reduce the likelihood of capsizing, dragging the mooring, and experiencing excessively fast and large boom movements. A **mooring** is the anchor-line-buoy combination used to keep the boat out on the water while the boat is not in use.

Now we're ready to **rig** the sailboat. First, we install the **tiller** and **rudder** by sliding the **pintles** into the **gudgeons**.

Figure 29. Slide pintles into gudgeons to attach helm

On a sloop rig, the **jib** is the smaller of the two sails and is located closer to the bow. One prepares to hoist the jib by: attaching it to the **mainstay**, attaching the **jib halyard** to the jib, and readying the **jib sheets**. The jib is raised *after* the mainsail because a jib that catches wind will turn the boat out of irons, making the rigging process more difficult and has been known to cause capsizing at the mooring.

Figure 30. Raise jib after main

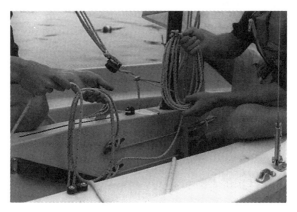

Figure 31. Coil extra line

We set up the **mainsail** by: attaching the **mainsail halyard** (hoisting line) to the top of the mainsail, raising the mainsail one-third of the way up the mast while mating the mainsail to the mast, and tying the front and back bottom corners to the mast and boom by using the **downhaul** and **outhaul** lines, respectively. The mainsail is then fully raised and the main halyard is tied, often to a cleat using the cleat hitch. We then fully raise the mainsail and tie off the main halyard to its cleat by tying a cleat hitch.

The last operation in the rigging process on a sloop rig is to hoist the jib. On a sloop rig, the jib halyard is hoisted and, like the main halyard, is secured to hold up its sail. In a single sail craft, the mainsail is simply hoisted and the main halyard is cleated.

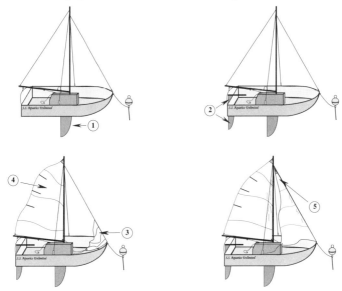

Figure 32. Rigging summary

On both sloop and lateen rig craft, the rigging process is completed by **coiling** extra line and securing all gear to the craft. At this point, the captain will instruct the crew on what their responsibilities include to sail the boat from the mooring, beach, or pier.

During the rigging process, the sails and boom must be free to move in order to keep the boat from moving and potentially capsizing. Sailors learn quickly that allowing sails and boom the freedom to move in the wind increases the potential of being struck by the boom and being whipped by the corner of the jib or other such sail. Experienced sailors learn to watch for wind gusts that cause sharp sail movement. Very stable craft (one that is heavy relative to the crew and gear weight) can be rigged without the centerboard lowered, which also helps maintain the boat's pointing into the wind. If the wind is sufficiently strong such that the sail and boom movement become dangerous, we can simply lower the sails and wait for the wind to diminish to a safer level.

Derigging is simply the reverse process of rigging; just lower the sails, remove the sails, remove the tiller and rudder, raise the centerboard or daggerboard, and unplug plugs if required.

Here are some general guidelines Crew members should remember when securing the craft after use: attach the main halyard to the end of the boom and hoist the boom until it is suspended horizontally over the boat, use the mainsheet to lock the boom over the center of the deck, stow equipment or removing it from the boat, dry then store sails away in a cool dry place, and coil extra line. A benefit of taking a few minutes for cleanup at the end of the sailing day is to make the rigging process easier next time, which will ultimately allow us to do more of what we want to be doing: *sailing*.

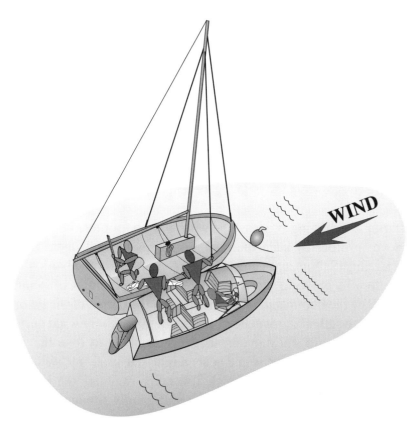

Figure 33. Securing the craft after use

Crew Theory
• Reading the wind

Sails catch wind; everyone knows that, but everyone might *not* know how to **read the wind**.

Wetting one's finger is generally *not* regarded as a proper method for determining wind direction. The wind tends to swirl around the sails, persons, and other objects on the sailboat, making the wind feel as though it is coming from a direction it is not.

By using our basic senses, we can more accurately **determine wind direction**.

Figure 34. Inaccurate method to determine wind direction

Using our basic senses:
- We can *see* the wind as **cat's-paws,** or dark spots, moving in the direction the wind is blowing across the water.
- We can *see* trees bending in the direction of the wind.
- We can *see* moored boats pointing into the direction from which the wind is coming.
- We can *feel* the wind cool our skin.
- We can *listen* to wind by facing into it and hearing the wind equally in both ears. This is known as **fine tuning**.

Figure 35. Hearing the wind to fine tune wind direction

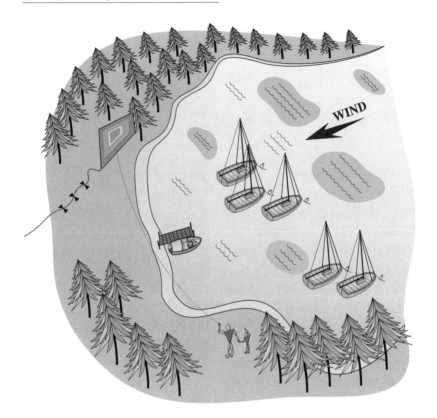

Figure 36. Determining wind direction on the water

Finally, when describing wind, we indicate the direction from which the wind is coming. For example, "Today, the wind is coming from there."

Figure 37. Indicating wind direction

Crew Practical

- Making the sailboat move w/o a paddle
- Stopping excessive heeling
- Basic Rule of the Road

The crew member's primary responsibility during actual sailing is to aid with boat balance and jib control. In general, we would like to keep the boat sailing flat on the water and to have the jib sail full with wind. To help keep the boat flat, the crew member may sit on port or starboard and may find him or herself crossing sides to achieve keeping the hull flat on the water. The crew member operates the jib by pulling in or easing the jib sheets, which travel through a pulley before attaching to the sail.

During normal sailing conditions, the captain sits on the windward side of the craft and keeps his or her attention forward. The captain chooses a stationary point toward which to sail. The captain's bow hand controls the mainsheet and stern hand controls the tiller. During this exercise, we simply try to keep the sails full and sail a straight course using *slight* tiller adjustments.

Figure 38. Sailing a straight course

Sailboat capsizing is the most common fear among inexperienced sailors, so let's learn three techniques to control the tilting of the sailboat, which sailors refer to as **heeling**, caused by excessive wind pressure on the sails:

1. Put more weight on the windward side.
2. Spill wind by letting the sails out (sheeting out).
3. Turn the boat into the wind using our steering wheel, the tiller.

Often, a combination of two or three methods will be required to control heeling.

Figure 39. Heeling

Figure 40. Weight controlling heeling

Figure 41. Tiller controlling heeling

Figure 42. Combination heel control

Now that we know what we will do once we are controlling the craft, we need to learn the proper method to take over the helm. Before transferring the mainsheet and tiller, the captain should choose a course and let the crew know the point on shore toward which the craft should sail to stay on that course. After letting out the mainsail to reduce heeling potential during transfer, we take the mainsheet with our bow hand and slide beside the captain to take control of the tiller. Good sailors watch for cat's-paws prior and during the transition to protect against unexpected heeling and loss of balance. At this point, we should simply develop a feel for how to maintain a straight sailing course. The tiller and mainsail should be transferred back to the more experienced sailor before turning the boat. Note that learning to control the mainsail and tiller can also be done in two steps (i.e., controlling the tiller while the captain controls the mainsheet and vice-versa).

When many boats are using the same waterway, there is often occasion to cross paths with other craft. Like automobiles, boats have rules of the road. As crew members, we need only remember, the **Basic Rule of the Road** is *avoid collisions!* (especially important if you are the smaller of the two craft!)

Figure 43. Avoid collisions

Crew Knots

- **Cleat hitch**
- **Figure 8 knot**

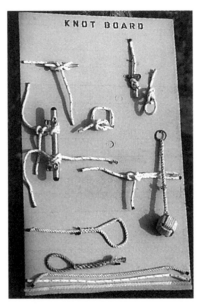

Figure 44. Sailor's knot board

Marlinspike seamanship, commonly known as ropework, is essential in sailing since so much rigging depends on lines. First, a piece of line has two ends: a **standing end**, which remains fixed, and a **running end,** which will be moving in our hands. As good sailing crew members, we should be proficient at tying the knots used in the rigging process, namely the cleat hitch and figure 8 knot.

The **cleat hitch** is used to tie off lines like the halyard and outhaul. Here we go: begin with a circle, next your X, complete with an underhand turn such that the running end runs parallel to the line beneath it.

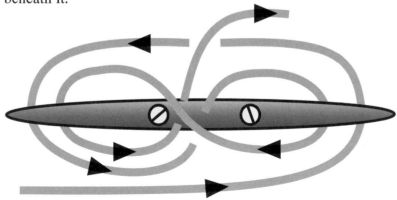

Figure 45. Cleat hitch illustration

Figure 46. Cleat hitch photo

The **figure 8 knot** is a stopper knot used for rigging to prevent the end of a line, such as the mainsheet, from slipping through its pulleys. To tie the figure 8 knot, we simply turn the running end around the standing end one-and-a-half times until we can see a figure 8. We complete this knot by guiding the running end through the loop not encircling the standing end. The figure 8 knot can always be taken out by simply "breaking it" by pushing the loop around the standing end of the figure 8 so that the line passing through that loop slides through the loop, which loosens the knot.

standing end

running end

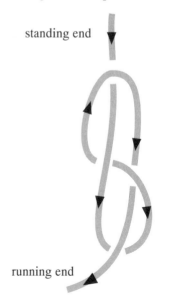

Figure 47. Figure 8 knot illustration   *Figure 48. Figure 8 knot photo*

Crew Review

1. We discussed the importance of wearing a Type II or Type III PFD. Describe the safety qualities of each type of PFD and give two or more examples of unexpected situations which would make you realize that wearing your PFD whenever you are boating is a pretty good idea.

2. List three pieces of safety equipment discussed in the Crew section and give one situation for each one's use. Now name two items not discussed which could also be used as safety equipment - be creative.

3. Sailboat nomenclature (names of parts of the boat) is a sailor's most important communication tool. Sketch a sailboat, then work from bow to stern and list as many parts of the sailboat as you can.

4. Why do we "shift our weight" when boarding any craft?

5. To make a floating craft more stable during the rigging process, we suggest lowering the centerboard or daggerboard and installing the rudder. Why do we recommend raising the jib after the mainsail and allowing the sails to swing free while rigging the sailboat?

6. (a) Give three or more examples of determining wind direction. (b) How do we describe wind direction to others?

7. (choose the correct words) During normal sailing conditions (not light wind conditions), the captain sits on the windward / leeward side and keeps his or her attention forward / backward. The captain's bow hand controls the mainsheet / tiller, and stern-hand controls the mainsheet / tiller.

8. Crew members help the more experienced sailing member(s) on the craft control excessive heeling by moving to the windward side, if necessary. What additional actions could the person at the helm perform if moving weight to windward were not enough to control excessive heeling?

9. Boating accidents are a serious concern to experienced sailors. What is the Basic Rule of the Road?

10. Name one line that requires tying off with the cleat hitch? Tie a cleat hitch. Name one line that requires tying off with the figure 8 knot? Tie a figure 8 knot.

Bonus: Using only one hand, tie a cleat hitch and a figure 8 knot.

We're now one step closer to making Sailing a Breeze!

2nd Mate Tools

- Standing & running rigging
- Nomenclature
- Parts of the sail
- Care of the sails
- Reefing the sail

As Crew members, we learned enough to assist more experienced sailors set up and operate the sailboat. As 2nd Mates, we will be learning to control the helm under supervision throughout all phases of a normal sailing day. This means our communication skills on the craft must be expanded, so we will now put some new nomenclature into our toolbox.

Figure 49. Standing rigging: shrouds

Rigging is classified as standing or running. **Standing rigging** refers to the wires and associated fittings which support the mast and provide means for attaching and supporting certain sails, such as the jib. Some common standing rigging parts are the shrouds, mainstay, and turnbuckles.

Figure 50. Standing rigging: mainstay

Figure 51. Standing rigging: chainplate

Running rigging refers to the lines and associated fittings used to hoist and control the sails. Some common running rigging parts are the sheets, halyards, and blocks. The mainsheet and jib sheet control the mainsail and jib, respectively. The sheets travel through blocks (i.e., a sailor's word for pulley) on their routes between a sailor's hand and their associated sails. Running the sheets through the blocks provides mechanical advantage over the sails, which is necessary for controlling the sails when the sails are exposed to the wind.

Figure 52. Running rigging: halyards

Figure 53. Running rigging: blocks

The running rigging lines are good applications for the cleat hitch and figure 8 knot. The main and jib halyards hold up the sails through the use of cleats found near the base of the mast. The figure 8 knot is always tied at the ends of the sheets and halyards to prevent these lines from slipping through their respective blocks in the event one loses grip of these lines. (This discussion is an example of how important sailboat nomenclature can be.)

Figure 54. Running rigging: sheets

To this point, we have learned many sailboat hardware names. As one would expect, a sailboat's sails also have special names to refer to their various parts and areas, so let's add some *sail* nomenclature to our growing toolbox.

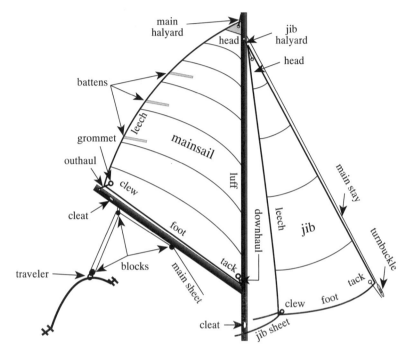

Figure 55. Sail nomenclature

The *top* of the sail is known as the **head**; this is the part to which the halyard is attached. The part of the mainsail along the mast is known as the **luff**. When the luff flutters back and forth, the sail is said to be *luffing*. The bottom corner where the mast and boom meet is referred to as the **tack** - this can be remembered by thinking that the sail is *tacked* down to the point where the mast and boom meet. The bottom edge along the boom is called the **foot**, on which the sail *stands*. The back corner is the **clew** - if it had a *clew*, it would be closer to the mast. The slanted edge is the **leech** - it is *leeching* onto the rest of the sail. Also, some sails contain **battens** to help the sail retain sail shape. Battens are generally made of wood or fiberglass.

Reefing the mainsail can make set up and storage a simpler task. One method for reefing the mainsail along the boom is the following. First, lower the mainsail. Then, fold and roll the dry sail such that its head is left exposed for quick set up. The mainsail is now held on top of the mast. Note that the mainsail's foot has remained in its rigged configuration. Next, the main halyard is disconnected from the mainsail head, attached to the end of the boom. The mainsheet is pulled through its block at **mid-ship** on

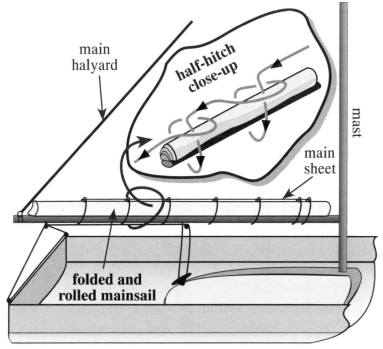

Figure 56. Reefed sail illustration

the boom so that no slack is left along the boom and the mainsheet lays untangled on the deck. The mainsheet is now cleated such that there is just enough slack to allow the boom to be hoisted parallel to the deck. Using the spare length of mainsheet, we secure the mainsail to the boom using a series of half-hitches spaced apart approximately two feet (0.6 meters). An initial wrap around the mainsail and boom directly above the cleat, then a clove hitch around the mast and boom to get started with the series of mast-to-stern clove hitches, is one technique sailors use for reefing. The running end of the mainsheet can be secured with a clove hitch and two half-hitches. At this point, the mainsail should be neatly secured to the boom, and the boom should be locked in place parallel to the deck and directly over the keel-line. Finally, the jib can be raised and wrapped around the mainstay (wind permitting) and secured with the jib sheet, or the jib can be derigged and stored in a cool dry place. Remember, a wet sail mildews, so take into account the weather between sailboat usages before reefing the sails.

Figure 57. Reefed sail

In addition to knowing the names of the parts and areas of sails, good 2nd Mate sailors should be familiar with the proper maintenance and **care of sails**. If a sail is wet, it should be hung in a cool, dry area until it is dry. Storing away a wet sail causes mildew to grow on the sail; **mildew** discolors and weakens sails. A dry sail can be folded and stored in a **sailbag**. Also, a dry sail can be reefed. It should be noted that ultraviolet light from the sun will, over time, weaken materials from which sails are made. So, if a sail is hung to dry in the sun, it should be put away once completely dry. Care should be taken to roll rather than fold a transparent vinyl or mylar window area if the sail is so equipped. Folding the window will leave a permanent translucent mark on it and look aesthetically unpleasing.

2nd Mate Theory

- Seed Theory
- Slot Effect

If you learn one concept from these lessons, the following theory of what makes a sailboat move should be it. The question we always ask our students is, "What makes an airplane go up?" Well, it has to do with the shape of the wings and the forces created as the velocity of wind increases across them. The tops of the wings are curved and tapered; the bottoms of the wings are flat. Since air striking the wing separates and rejoins at the other edge of the wing at the same time, the air traveling above the wings must flow faster than the air traveling below the wing because of the longer path the air above the wing must travel in the same time period. This increased wind speed displaces air molecules above the wings, which creates a low pressure area, or virtual vacuum. The wings are pulled up to fill the displaced air molecule void, and, since the wings are attached to the airplane, the plane goes up.

Figure 58. Windflow analogy

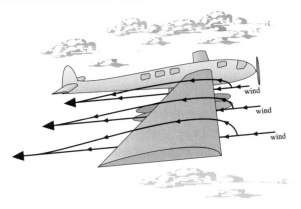

Figure 59. Wind flow across airplane wings

So how does flying relate to sailing? Look at our sail - curved like an airplane wing. The sail will develop *its* low pressure area behind it (on the leeward side of the sail); and, since the sail is connected to the mast - and the mast to the hull - the boat moves. A well-shaped sail can provide as much as 80% pull. (Of course, a sailboat headed downwind with its sails sheeted out over the gunwale will rely on the wind to push the sails.) A jib will increase sail area, but it will also increase the rate at which wind passes behind the mainsail. We will refer to the low pressure phenomenon on the leeward side of the sails as the **slot effect**.

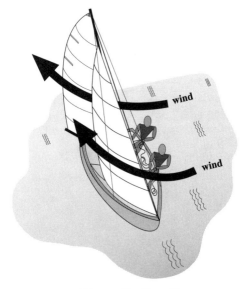

Figure 60. Slot effect

The other forces acting on a sailboat can be described by what we will call the **seed theory**. We just finished discussing that the sail pulls the boat when sailing across the wind, and, since the sails rarely directly face the bow, the craft should travel diagonally forward. However, because the boat has vertical parts beneath the water (i.e., the centerboard, hull, and rudder), the boat will resist sideward motion; this resistance to sideward travel is referred to as **lateral resistance**. Lateral resistance works against the forces trying to move the sailboat sideways. The squeezing of the hull by the forces trying to move the craft sideways and the forces resisting the sideward movement results in the craft going *forward* because of the shape of the hull; that is, the tapered shape of the bow offers the path of least resistance. In other words, like a watermelon seed being *shot out* when squeezed between one's fingers.

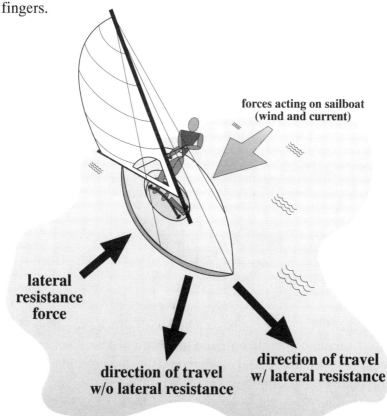

forces acting on sailboat
(wind and current)

lateral
resistance
force

direction of travel
w/o lateral resistance

direction of travel
w/ lateral resistance

Figure 61. Seed theory

2nd Mate Practical

- Points of sail
- Coming about
- Jibing
- Getting out of irons
- Getting underway & landing
- Capsizing
- Trimming sails and hulls
- Rules of the Road

Now that we understand the forces that make a sailboat move, let us attach names to a sailboat's direction of movement in relation to the direction of the wind. When the bow of the boat points directly into the wind, the boat is said to be in **irons**. In irons, the boat cannot move because the wind passes equally fast on both sides of the sail. A **beat**, or **close haul**, is the closest sailing direction to the wind. A **reach** describes moving across the wind. We have a **close reach**, a **beam reach** (when the wind travels across the widest part of the boat, or **beam of the boat**), and a **broad reach** or **far reach**. A **run** describes moving directly away from the wind, remembered as *running* away from the wind.

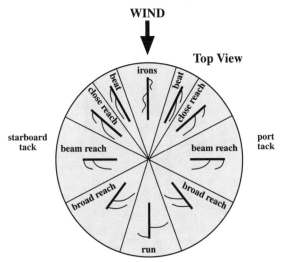

Figure 62. Points of sail

The other two sailing direction labels with which every 2nd Mate sailor should be familiar are the starboard and port tacks. If the wind first strikes the boat on starboard, the boat is said to be on a **starboard tack**. Similarly, if the wind first strikes the boat on port, the boat is said to be on a **port tack**. The best way to remember the names given to the points of sail is to work them into your conversation while enjoying your sailing day.

When sailing on any point of sail, the captain is responsible for trimming the sails and hull. **Trimming a sail** means to find the sail's optimum or most airplane wing-like shape. Trimming the sail is performed by **sheeting out** the sail until it begins to luff. A sail is said to be **luffing** when its front edge, the luff, flutters back and forth; the fluttering may be slow and gentle or fast and rippled. The sail sheet is **sheeted in** (pulled in) until the luffing stops and the sail is smooth and full. For a craft with both a jib and mainsail, the jib is trimmed first. A mainsail experiencing a **backwind effect** (caused by a jib sheeted in too much as a result of an improper trim) is often mistaken as being a mainsail that is luffing, which can lead to a poor trim on the mainsail. As 2nd Mates, we must learn to distinguish between jib-caused backwind and wind-caused luffing. The cure for backwind is to first re-trim the jib and then the mainsail.

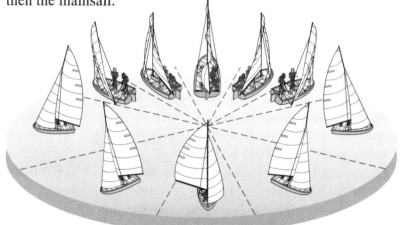

Figure 63. Points of sail, 3-dimensional

Sails are trimmed at different angles as a function of the point of sail. These angles can be generalized. The closer to the wind one sails, the closer to the keel line the boom will be angled when the mainsail is trimmed; the farther from the wind one sails, the farther from the keel-line the boom will be angled when trimmed. Students find it interesting that sheeting very far out in extremely light wind conditions when on a beam reach is necessary to help the craft to move forward. This is necessary because light winds need help in making the turn around the mast to properly affect the sail leaning the boat to leeward will also make the sail form a curve under its own weight.

Trimming the hull is performed by adjusting *weight* on the boat. One must develop a sense of hull balance over time, but again, just enough lateral resistance to prevent sideslipping is what the captain tries to achieve by trimming the hull.

Figure 64. Trimming sails

Sailing a lateen rig craft will help make the concept of trimming the hull clear. One will find that on moderate and heavy wind days, the daggerboard, rudder, and natural heel will offer enough lateral resistance to allow the hull to be kept flat

Figure 65. Trimming hull

without sideslipping. On very light wind days, the sideward force of the wind against the hull will be little so the lateral resistance against the rudder and daggerboard results in little counteracting force. The end result is that artificially heeling the hull to prevent sideslipping will be necessary.

These discussions on sheeting out the sail and inducing a heel on the hull on very light wind days may seem counter-intuitive, which is why we encourage our students to challenge themselves to sail on days when hardly a ripple can be seen on the water.

Question: How often does sail & hull trimming occur?
Answer: Continuously.

When sailing in a confined area, such as a lake or bay, we often have the need to change sailing tacks. Changing the sailing **tack** is accomplished in one of two ways: coming about or jibing.

When the *bow* crosses through the wind from starboard to port or port to starboard tack, the sailboat is said to have **come about**.

Figure 66. Coming about

Before coming about, the captain calls, "Prepare to come about!" The crew responds, "ready!" The captain points the tiller all the way to leeward after calling, "Come about, **hard-a-lee**!" *The captain and crew keep their heads down to avoid being struck by the boom.*

To keep his or her attention forward, the captain exchanges the tiller and mainsheet by using a behind-the-back pass. In the case of a sloop rig, the crew should continue to hold the jib sheet *taut* until the sailboat has passed completely *through irons* before beginning jib control with the new leeward-side

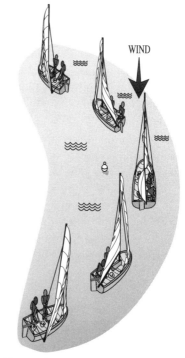

Figure 67. Coming about illustration

jib sheet; the brief period the jib experiences backwind is intended to get the sailboat to cross easily and efficiently through irons. The sails and hull are trimmed once underway on the new tack. Note that coming about is generally performed when one wishes to change sailing tacks and continue to travel upwind or simply to change beam reach tacks.

When the captain wishes to change the boat's tack and sail downwind, the captain performs a jibe. During the **jibe** exercise, the stern crosses through the wind as the sailing tack changes from port to starboard or starboard to port.

The captain calls, "Prepare to jibe!" before jibing, to alert the crew. The captain calls, "Jibe Ho!", and the mainsail is pulled in over the craft and helped across in conjunction with the captain's pointing the tiller to windward.

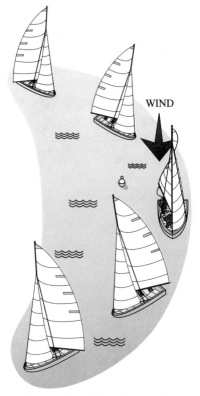

WIND

Figure 68. Jibing illustration

During this entire exercise, *the captain and crew keep their heads down to avoid being struck by the boom.* Because of his or her need for quick response when jibing, the captain may want to switch the tiller and mainsheet using the behind-the-back pass before performing the jibe. After the jibe, the sails and hull are trimmed once sailing underway on the new tack.

Figure 69. Goosewing jibe

A **goosewing jibe** describes the case when the boom gets lifted up and slammed across the hull. A goosewing jibe can occur because of a sudden wind-shift or by a captain's mistake. *Goosewing jibes are dangerous for both sailors and craft and should be avoided!*

Now that we know the names for the points of sail, methods for trimming the sails and hull, and skills to change sailing tacks by coming about and jibing, let's put this all together by sailing on a triangular, clockwise sailing course. Starting from downwind, we can sail upwind on a close reach or beat and perform a series of tack changes; each upwind tack change is accomplished by coming about. We then bear off and sail downwind on a broad reach. To get back to the starting point, we must change tacks by jibing, then continue on a broad reach or run, depending on the course. Each point of sail requires constant trimming of sails and hull and the triangular course allows us to practice both coming about and jibing. Once becoming comfortable with sailing the course clockwise, we should sail the course counter-clockwise.

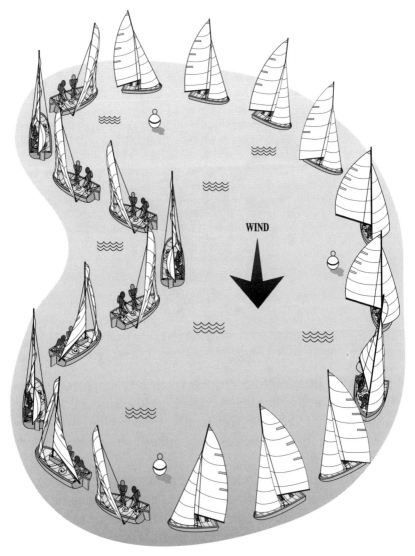

Figure 70. Coming about and jibing exercise: the triangular course

Getting stuck in irons can be frustrating, so let's learn **how to get out of irons**. When a sailboat is in irons, the boat points directly into the wind and, consequently, wind passes equally fast past both sides of the sail(s). The trick to getting one's craft out of irons is to re-establish the sailboat's point of sail in order to get the sails to stay smooth and full. The methods sailors use to turn the craft out of irons are different for sloop and lateen rig craft.

Figure 71. Irons - backwind jib

On a sloop rig craft, we can take advantage of the jib in helping us get out of irons. **Backwinding the jib** by using the jib sheet, we can simply wait for the wind to push the jib, which turns the craft out of irons. This jib sheet control is similar to the coming about exercises in that the windward side jib sheet is held taught and the jib experiences backwinding until the craft is no longer in irons.

When sailing a lateen rig that has only the single sail to turn the craft out of irons, the captain must **backwind the mainsail** by physically moving the boom over his or her head. When the boom is held in this position, the sail will take-on its airplane wing-like shape. This shape will start the boat's moving forward and allow the captain to steer out of

Figure 72. Backwind mainsail

irons by simply using the tiller. Once moving ahead on a new point of sail, the mainsail can be carefully released and mainsheet control of the mainsail can begin again.

If the boat is being held in irons by very strong winds, the boat may actually begin to travel backward through the water. Being forced backward by the wind when held in irons is mainly experienced by light planing hull craft like lateen rigs. Captains in this scenario can use the rudder like a steering wheel in conjunction with backwinding the mainsail. Here, the captain backwinds the mainsail while holding the tiller away from him or herself. The rudder steers the stern diagonally backward while the

Figure 73. Use tiller and mainsail

mainsail uses the wind to steer the bow diagonally forward in the other direction. These two directions combine to spin the craft out of irons. Once the boat begins to turn out of irons, a gentle pull on the tiller to windward will set the boat firmly on its new sailing course. This move should be practiced on moderate wind days before it is needed on heavy wind days to prevent the craft from being driven backward into rocks on shore.

By knowing how to get out of irons, we also know how to **get underway** from stationary positions, such as moorings, docks, and beaches. At any of these locations, the sailboat usually begins in irons to prevent it from being pushed into objects, capsizing, and damaging the craft or us. Since the craft is in irons, we can just apply the procedure for getting out of irons and the craft is underway. The trick is to start the boat on a tack such that the captain and crew do not need to quickly switch sides once getting underway.

Figure 74. Mooring approach

Figure 75. Mooring pickup

Moorings and **landings at piers** should always end up with the sailboat in irons to protect us and the craft. A basic technique for completing a *mooring* in irons is to pass the mooring approximately one boat length to the leeward then to head up into irons one and one-half boat lengths later. Because the wind is prone to shift, more than one mooring attempt may be necessary, so we lower the sails *only after* the boat has been secured to the mooring. Unlike floating moorings, docks and piers are stationary objects, so we must have very, very little forward momentum at the end of the approach. We recommend beginning the approach with the sails sheeted out to have less than optimum sail shape and, therefore, less than maximum momentum in case of distance misjudgement when heading up into irons.

Capsizing is dangerous, so a specific procedure should be followed if this should happen:
1. Save yourself.
2. Count heads to ensure everyone else's safety.
3. Swim the boat into irons.
4. Upright the boat by putting weight on the center or daggerboard.
5. Re-enter the craft one at a time.
6. Check everyone's physical condition, paying particular attention for signs of hypothermia and shock, and seek medical attention immediately, if necessary.

Figure 76. Save yourself - Mark calls, "One!"

Figure 77. Save yourself - Gary calls, "Two!"

Lowering the sails before trying to upright the sailboat may be necessary because of water weight on the sails. If the craft is difficult to upright, place the spare PFD at the top of the floating mast to prevent the boat from turtling. **Turtling** describes a capsized boat whose hull bottom is facing upward, giving the appearance of a swimming turtle. In the case of a turtled sailboat, the mast is pointing straight down making uprighting the capsized boat much more difficult, particularly if the mast gets lodged in sand, weeds, rocks, or mud. Getting the PFD down from the mast top is best left until the crew and craft are safely ashore.

Figure 78. Tie PFD to mast to avoid turtling

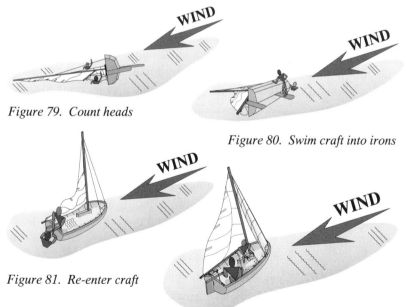

Figure 79. Count heads

Figure 80. Swim craft into irons

Figure 81. Re-enter craft

Figure 82. Bail craft and sail

Do not leave the craft except in an emergency. *A boat is much easier to spot than a lone swimmer.*

Rules of the Road: In general, the less maneuverable craft shall have the right of way. The following five rules apply:

1. A sailboat on a *starboard* tack has the right of way *over* a sailboat on a *port* tack.

2. The *leeward* boat has the right of way *over* the *windward* boat.

3. A boat *on* a tack has the right of way *over* a boat that is *changing* tack.

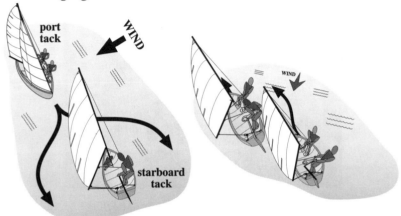

Figure 83. Starboard over port   *Figure 84. Leeward over windward*

4. **Slower** boats have the right of way *over faster*, overtaking boats.

5. **Less maneuverable** craft have the right of way *over more maneuverable* craft. A sailboat will usually have the right of way over powered vessels and paddle driven craft since a

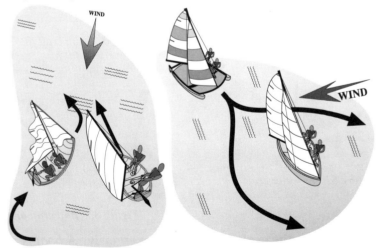

Figure 85. On over changing tack   *Figure 86. Slower over faster*

sailboat is dependent on the wind direction, making it less maneuverable than power or paddle driven craft. However, as bigger power boats have less maneuverability than smaller sailboats, smaller sailboats should be prepared to yield the right of way.

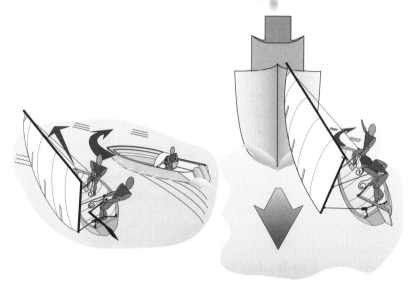

Figure 87. Sail over power   *Figure 88. More maneuverable over less maneuverable*

Remember, the basic rule of the road is avoid collisions.

Figure 89. Basic rule of the road: avoid collisions

Consult with the Coast Guard in the area you will be sailing to be sure you have all the current rules and regulations.

2nd Mate Knots

- **Clove hitch w/ 2 half hitches**
- **Bowline**
- **Square knot**

Now that we have advanced our sailing skills, we will find that we need knots used for more than just rigging the sailboat. The clove hitch, bowline, and square knot are three such knots that have many general purpose uses for sailors.

The **clove hitch**, simply two underhand loops (around-over-around-through), is useful for tying a boat to a pole and reefing the mainsail because the clove hitch will not slip while tension is applied. If tension is not to be applied continuously, two half-hitches should be added. Two **half-hitches** are made by making two overhand loops around the standing end.

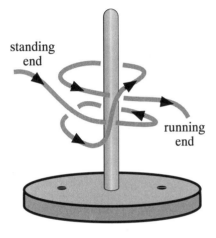

standing end

running end

Figure 90. Clove hitch illustration

Figure 91. Clove hitch photo

The **bowline** is used for making a temporary loop at the end of a line for uses such as a temporary dock line. To tie a bowline, one twists an overhand loop with the running end hand's thumb and forefinger. Then, with the running end, "the rabbit comes out of the hole, goes around the tree, and jumps back into the hole."

standing
end

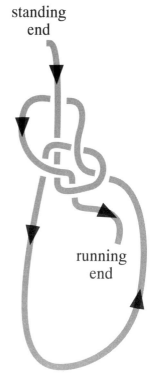

running
end

Figure 92. Bowline illustration

Figure 93. Bowline photo

Right over left, then left over right makes the **square knot** or **reef knot**. The square knot is used to tie a line around an object with the idea of easily being able to undo the knot holding it together. Many such line and knot configurations can be used to reef a sail.

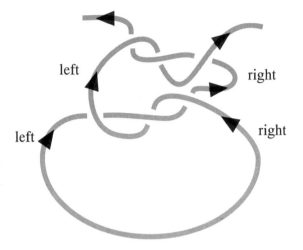

left

right

left

right

Figure 94. Square knot illustration

Figure 95. Square knot photo

2nd Mate Review

1. List two or more standing and running rigging parts.

2. (a) Sketch a sail, then name as many areas of the mainsail as you can.
(b) What phrases could be useful in remembering sail nomenclature?

3. (a) Describe one method of reefing a mainsail. (b) What might cause us to fold our mainsail and store it in a cool dry place rather than reefing it?

4. The slot effect suggests that sails are similar to airplane wings in that a low pressure area or virtual vacuum develops on the outside of the curved sail. What causes the low pressure area?

5. The seed theory suggests that a sailboat gets shot forward like a watermelon seed when squeezed between one's fingers. (a) What are the "fingers" in the case of the sailboat? (b) Why does the boat get shot *forward*?

6. Assume that your centerboard or daggerboard were no longer able to be used after an accidental capsize. How might you adjust for its loss?

7. (a) Draw a points of sail chart (circle) and lable the points of sail.
(b) The wind strikes the craft on which side when sailing on a port tack?

8. (a) How and why do we trim sails and hull? (b) How often do we trim?

9. (a) When coming about, the <u>bow / stern</u> is said to cross through irons.
(b) When jibing, the <u>bow / stern</u> is said to cross through irons.

10. Being trapped in irons means that the wind is passing equally fast on both sides of the sail, resulting in no forward travel. Without using the rudder, how does an experienced sailor get out of irons?

11. (a) Present the capsizing procedure you follow during a capsizing drill.
(b) Why should the boat point into irons *before* being uprighted? (c) Why should sailors stay with the capsized craft except in an emergency?

12. The five rules of the road were created to prevent accidents. (a) For each rule, prove to yourself that the "right of way" boat is indeed the less maneuverable craft. (b) Who can help you with the specific rules in your sailing area?

Bonus: Tie the clove hitch (w/ 2 half hitches), the bowline, and square knot three consecutive times. Now apply each in practice during your sailing day.

We're now one step closer to making Sailing a Breeze!

1st Mate Tools

- **Sailboat hardware**
- **Protect & repair materials**
- **Types of line**
- **Anchors & moorings**

If we're going to be good practical sailors, we should know the various **hardware** found on a sailboat. By knowing sailboat hardware, we can repair our craft and also modify its performance.

To begin, metals used in making items like blocks, chainplates, and anchors should be water and preferably salt water compatible so the sailboat hardware does not rust. Popular metals used to make sailboat parts are stainless steel, galvanized steel, and silicon-bronze.

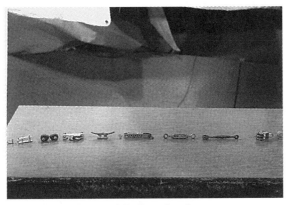

Figure 96. Boat hardware

Blocks, whose common names are pulleys, are used to guide sheets and other lines to provide sailors with mechanical advantage over that to which these guided lines are attached. Some blocks have ball bearings for turning ease and quick response. Examples of places where blocks can be found on the sailboat are: on the boom and traveler for the mainsheet, inside the mast for the main and jib halyards, and on the starboard and port gunwales for guiding the jib sheets.

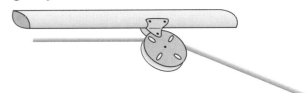

Figure 97. Boat hardware - Blocks

Sailors often use turnbuckles and chainplates in their shrouds and mainstay connections to the gunwales. A **turnbuckle** is often made of three parts. The center can be spun to screw or unscrew both outer segments at the same time; this mechanical action effectively lengthens or shortens the turnbuckle. A **chainplate** is lengthened or shortened by moving the pin passing through sets of holes on each plate.

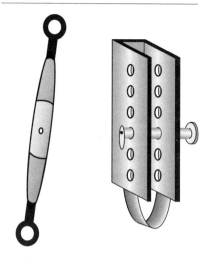

Figure 98. Boat hardware - turnbuckle and chainplate

Turnbuckles and chainplates allow sailors to adjust mainstay tension to control the mast position forward or back and the shroud tension to control the mast's lean from side to side. Advanced sailors use the turnbuckle and chainplate adjustment capabilities to fine tune a sailboat's response to the wind.

Clevis and cotter pins are two more examples of boat hardware with which all 1st Mates should be aware. The **clevis pin** is a solid, smooth metal pin with a wide head on one end and either a hole or spring released pin at the other end. The **cotter pin** is often a straight or circular thick, durable wire that fits through the clevis pin hole. The cotter pin is used to keep the clevis pin securely in position.

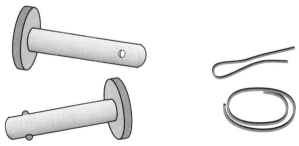

Figure 99. Boat hardware - clevis & cotter pins

Clevis and cotter pins are useful in turnbuckle and chainplate setups. A metal ring at the base of a mainstay and shroud are inserted into the chainplate. The clevis pin is then inserted through the chainplate's side holes, passing through the metal ring in-between. The combination of the clevis pin head and cotter pin holds the clevis pin in the chainplate, which keeps the mainstay and shrouds in the chainplates, which holds the mast in the vertical position allowing us to sail.

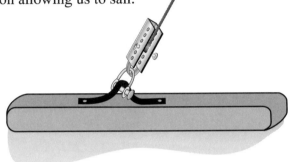

Figure 100. Chainplate and shroud setup

Cleats come in many different sizes and styles. Some popular styles include standard cleats, cleats with an eye, jam cleats, and cam cleats.

The **traditional cleat** allows for tying a cleat hitch to it. A **cleat with an eye** is a traditional cleat but with a hole in its base large enough to insert a line formed in a loop. The loop can then encircle the cleat.

Figure 101. Traditional cleat   *Figure 102. Cleat with eye*

A **jam cleat** allows for a line to be slid through in only one direction. The jam cleat holds the line until released by pulling the line up and out. A **cam cleat** often has two moving parts that allow a line to be slid through in one direction, but the teeth on the turning parts prevent the line from sliding back through in the other direction. One must lift the line up and out of the cam cleat to release it from the cam cleat's teeth. The cam cleat is often used to hold the main and jib sheets, which is fine if constant sail trimming is not desired and no wind gusts are foreseeable that might require immediate sheeting out of the sails.

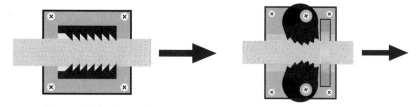

Figure 103. Jam cleat   *Figure 104. Cam cleat*

Shackles are handy items to use when working with eyes (in mooring lines and standing rigging wires) and grommets (in sails). Shackles are essentially a clevis and cotter pin arrangements that come with their own supporting frames. When the shackle's clevis pin is inserted (often by screwing it into a socket),

the shackle forms a closed, oval-like shape. Large shackles often allow for a wire to be inserted through the clevis pin head, then twisted around the shackle to keep the clevis pin from unscrewing.

Figure 105. Shackle

Grommets are metal rings put into sails to form an eye, which enables sailors to rig the sails without tearing the sail material. Grommets often come in two parts and require a special tool to put them together.

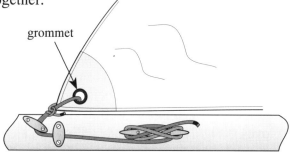

grommet

Figure 106. Grommet

Thimbles are often used for making a stiff loop (referred to by sailors as an eye) in lines or standing rigging wires. **Thimbles** are usually constructed of metal or thick synthetic materials and are teardrop shaped. Thimbles are generally cupped one half of the line or wire diameter so that the line or wire firmly remains wrapped around the thimble.

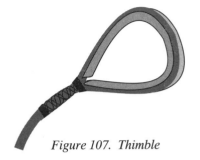

Figure 107. Thimble

Besides knowing boat hardware, 1st Mate sailors should be familiar with **protection and repair materials**. Fiberglass, marine putty, and paints are three such items we might find ourselves using with some regularity.

Figure 108. Repair materials

Fiberglass is an important material for protecting and repairing fiberglass and wooden craft. Two items are required for fiberglass repair - fiberglass cloth and fiberglass resin. Always wear a respiratory mask while working with fiberglass resin, as the vapors may be harmful. Follow the manufacturer's directions, mix the resin and catalyst, and combine the mix with the fiberglass cloth. Apply a few layers to the surface being repaired. Make sure that air bubbles are worked out as well as possible. A pair of protective gloves is highly recommended. Epoxies are used for similar purpose and require similar mixing of resin and catalyst.

Marine putty is an invaluable general purpose repair material. Simply mix as specified in the manufacturer's directions and apply. Because putty surfaces become very hard after drying, putty surfaces that are unsmooth before drying will be covered with sharp burrs. Therefore, try to make the putty surface smooth, so post-drying sanding of burrs is minimized.

Paints are used to protect boats from weathering, algae, plant life, and, in the case of a boat to be used in saltwater, barnacles from attaching themselves to the hull. Most marine stores carry topside paints and bottomside paints. The paints available are quite diverse, so it is important to understand the particular paint's qualities and intended uses before putting it on your craft. Marine paints tend to be expensive, making it worthwhile to spend the time in getting the right paint the first time. Some factors to consider when deciding on bottomside paints are: water type (fresh or salt), boat speed, period between boat usages, hull construction material, age of hull, and cost. Like other repair materials, follow manufacturer's directions during application of paints.

In addition to the protect and repair materials discussed, sailors have the dubious pleasure of working with other items, such as woods, like teak, suited for marine usage (and the associated oils, stains, and varnishes that go along with woods), adding things like handrails, boat bumpers, anchor chocks, signal lights, bilge pumps, sail repair kits, sail bleaches, and many other miscellaneous items that can be added to and are important for maintaining a boat's aesthetics and performance. Browsing marine store shelves can be quite enlightening in terms of learning about these items and other protection and repair materials. In fact, many sailors find that after learning how to maintain and repair their boat, they enjoy keeping their boat in shape as much as they enjoy sailing it.

Line is rope cut for a purpose. The different types of line often used in sailing are: manila, nylon, dacron, and polypropylene.

manila

nylon

dacron

polypropylene

Figure 109. Lines: manila, nylon, dacron, and polypropylene

Manila, which is often used for moorings and anchors, costs less than synthetics, but is rough on the hands. Manila line wears from sand and long periods of wetness.

Nylon is a very popular synthetic line because of its strength, flexibility, softness, resistance to mildew and abrasion. Nylon is good for anchor and mooring lines because its stretch quality provides shock-absorption. This same stretch quality makes nylon poor material for sheets and halyards.

Dacron, another synthetic line, has a low stretch quality and retains full strength when wet, making dacron a good choice for sheets and halyards. Dacron, like nylon, is flexible, soft, and resistant to mildew and abrasion.

Polypropylene is another low stretch synthetic line, but polypropylene is more susceptible to abrasion than nylon or dacron. Because polypropylene floats very well, its best use is as a floating line, such as a waterskiing line or mooring pickup.

When **caring for lines**, swishing or shaking a line in the water to clean sand and other foreign debris from it works well as a cleaning method. Using a high pressure hose tends to force sand deeper into the line, causing the line to weaken. Sand and other particles weaken line because their microscopic, sharp edges wear and cut the small fibers from which a line is made. The best method for maintaining a clean, strong line is by keeping it on clean, dry surfaces. Today's lines can take a lot of abuse, but regular inspection and replacement of lines that exhibit wear, mildew, or general aging is recommended to keep the sailboat, anchor, mooring, and dock lines functional and safe.

As good 1st Mate sailors, we should be familiar with some basic anchors, understand how they work, and bring one along when sailing. The type of anchor used should be based on waterway bottom conditions, boat displacement, wind conditions, wave conditions, and current strength.

Figure 110. Danforth and mushroom anchors

Two common **anchor types** are the Danforth and mushroom anchors. The **Danforth anchor**, lightweight and good for most bottom conditions, works by its spades wedging themselves beneath debris on the water's bottom or dig themselves into sand and thick mud. When using a Danforth anchor, one should attach a second, lighter trip line (floated to the surface with a buoy). This **trip line** should be attached to the anchor in such a way that it will back out the anchor from under whatever it has lodged itself. Otherwise, depending on current strength, line length, water depth, and hull weight, having to cut or release the anchor line may be one's only choice to free the craft from the lodged anchor.

The **mushroom anchor**, which works well in sand and mud bottom conditions, uses the principle of suction; that is, a mushroom anchor can provide many times greater holding force than its weight when it is settled beneath sand or mud. Heavy mushroom anchors are often used for permanent moorings.

Whatever type of anchor one uses, one must always be sure to use an **anchor rode** (anchor line of a small boat) capable of handling the weight of the craft. The strength of line (rated by tensile strength in pounds or kilograms) needed for the mooring line should be able to suspend five times the boat's weight, and more if the presence of waves is expected. In addition, the length of the anchor line should be five to ten times the depth of the water. Two or more anchors can be used in conjunction from the bow and stern to keep the boat from swinging, causing lifting and displacement of only a single anchor. We recommend talking to experienced sailors in the areas you will be sailing to learn of the water's bottom characteristics and good anchoring techniques for that location.

Figure 111. Anchoring

1st Mate Theory

• True and apparent wind

By better understanding the wind and its interaction with a moving sailboat, we will become better sailors because we will know how to trim our sails more effectively. To start, we must first be familiarized with the difference between true and apparent wind. To do so, we need three definitions:

1. **True Wind:** The wind we feel as a result of air moving relative to our standing still. True wind is the moving air we commonly refer to as wind; it is the wind that blows a hat off one's head and the wind that creates the moving cat's-paws on the water's surface.

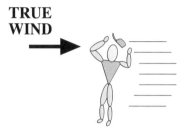

Figure 112. True Wind

2. **Wind of Movement:** The wind we feel as a result of moving relative to stationary air. An analogy can be drawn between a moving sailboat and a person running: as the runner moves faster, the runner feels more wind against his or her face from the increased speed. This can be visualized by a hat that flies backward off one's head when running.

Figure 113. Wind of Movement

3. **Apparent Wind:** The wind we feel as a result of combining the True Wind and the Wind of Movement. The wind will *appear* to be blowing from a 45° angle if the runner runs equally as fast as the True Wind blowing directly at his or her side.

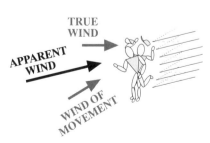

Figure 114. Apparent Wind

Remember, not only do *we* feel the apparent wind, but so do our sails! Thus, *because we sail by the apparent wind*, the sail(s) must be trimmed continuously to account for the varying True Wind *and* the boat's associated Wind of Movement. Does this change our method for trimming the sails? Certainly not. Because the sails automatically monitor the True Wind and Wind of Movement - known now as Apparent Wind and the sail's point of luffing is determined by that Apparent Wind, we have already learned to sail by the Apparent Wind. Remember, we learned to trim the sails by sheeting out until we observe some luffing, then sheeting in until the sails are smooth and full. So now we know that the faster our sailboat moves over the water, the closer to the keel-line the sail will be located when properly trimmed. Keep in mind, however, that the points of sail chart defines names of the sailboat's sailing direction relative to the True Wind. This suggests that even though our point of sail is a beam reach, the boat's forward speed might be fast enough to require the sail trim of a close reach. *Very interesting.*

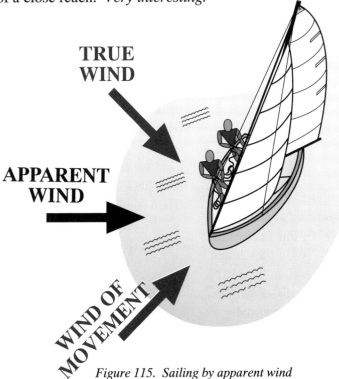

TRUE WIND

APPARENT WIND

WIND OF MOVEMENT

Figure 115. Sailing by apparent wind

1st Mate Practical

* Wing & wing
* Light wind conditions
* Person overboard
* Artificial respiration

As 1st Mate sailors, we should begin to develop our finer sailing skills by practicing a new skill, wing & wing, and sailing in a deceptively challenging wind condition: light wind. The wing & wing skill will develop our fine feel for both the wind on our sails and our tiller correction control. Sailing in light wind conditions will require us to develop both our sail and hull trimming skills and fine feel for the wind direction.

A **wing & wing** describes being on a run point of sail but having the mainsail all the way over one side of the craft and the jib all the way over the other. Be very careful because this balancing act is notorious for ending up in a goosewing jibe. When controlling the helm, we will find that the slightest movement of the tiller will upset the sails' harmony. Also, we will find that some hulls like to roll from side to side and that the centerboard may vibrate from the water passing across it. After developing the wing & wing skill, we can have the crew raise the centerboard to reduce the drag

it causes. **Drag** is a friction force, created between the sailboat and the water, that reduces forward momentum. Note that because we are sailing directly downwind, no lateral resistance is necessary. However, we must be aware that raising the centerboard will make the craft less stable, increasing capsizing potential. In addition to sailing wing & wing as a fine wind-feel skill practice, many sailors find sailing wing & wing both challenging and exciting.

Figure 116. Sailing wing & wing

Light wind conditions can be difficult even for experienced sailors. Go back to basics - concentrate on trimming the sails and hull. More often than not, one will find the craft can move when hardly a ripple exists on the water by sheeting the sail(s) well out over the side of the boat to make it easier for what little wind exists to get around the sail(s). And, in some planing hull craft, one will find that inducing a slight artificial heel on the hull by adding weight to the leeward side is necessary. This induced heel makes up for the lack of lateral resistance by the centerboard due to having little side pressure on the sails for the centerboard to counteract. Also, because planing hulls sit on top of the water rather than deep in the water like displacement hull craft without the artificially induced lateral resistance, the boat will either sit idly in the water or even sideslip. The captain who can sail in light wind conditions has an excellent feel for the wind and the sailboat.

Figure 117. Person overboard

A **person overboard** situation should be rehearsed in a controlled fashion. Before we begin, we must note that it is important to *always maintain visual contact with the overboard victim* during the entire practice drill and more important in the event of a real emergency. In addition, practicing with a buoy or spare PFD before attempting to rescue a real person simulating a victim is advised.

The following guide to a person overboard situation can be modified to suit one's particular situation. *First*, throw a flotation safety device to the victim and signal for help using audible and visual distress signals. *Second*, if the victim can reach the craft, stop the sailboat and wait. *Third*, if the craft must return for the victim, the procedure is to count to five after the person overboard fell out, perform a jibe, and approach the victim on a close reach. Wind conditions may be too strong to safely perform a jibe, so

Figure 118. Pickup overboard victim on windward side

coming about may be the preferred method for returning to the victim. *Fourth*, make contact with the victim such that the victim is on the windward side of the boat. The victim's being on the windward side will allow the captain to see the victim the entire

time and prevent accidental injury by the hull or boom in the event of a wind shift, wind gust, or distance misjudgment. The sails should be luffing well out over the leeward side of the boat when making contact with the victim; this is called the **safety position**. *Fifth*, steer the boat into irons and allow the sails to flutter freely until the overboard victim is safely in the boat. *Sixth*, aid the overboard victim while he or she re-enters the boat. The transom is generally a more stable

Figure 119. Re-enter craft over transom

re-entry point than the gunwales. IMPORTANT: only under emergency circumstances should another crew member enter the water, and then *only* with proper flotation safety equipment. It is always safer to extend the spare paddle from the safety of the craft rather than entering the water. *Seventh*, the rescued overboard sailor should be checked for signs of hypothermia and shock once safely rescued and seek medical attention, if necessary.

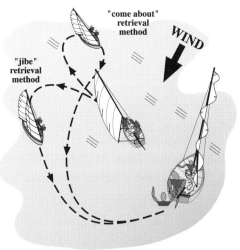

Figure 120. Person overboard illustration - come about and jibe methods

Artificial respiration knowledge lends itself well to sailing because of the potential danger found within the sport. As always, be prepared by knowing Red Cross standards, learning current medical artificial respiration techniques, and using common sense.

Figure 121. Be

Figure 122. prepared

Figure 123. for the

Figure 124. unexpected!

1st Mate Knots

- **Rolling hitch**
- **Sheet bend**

The **rolling hitch** is more dependable than a clove hitch because the rolling hitch tends to hold without constant tension being applied. The rolling hitch is tied by making two turns around the pole, overlapping the standing part on each turn. The rolling hitch is completed by making an underhand loop above the standing end. Two half-hitches can be added by making two overhand loops with the running end around the standing end to ensure the line stays wrapped around the pole.

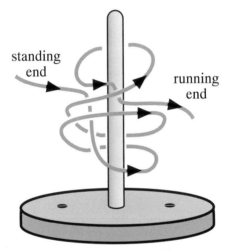

Figure 125. Rolling hitch illustration

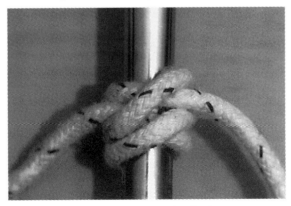

Figure 126. Rolling hitch photo

If we want to attach two different pieces of line, we should use the square knot's cousin, the **sheet bend**. We start the sheet bend by making a loop in one of the lines. Then, the running end of the second line comes up through the loop, wraps around the first line, and is weaved between the loop and the standing end of the second line. One application of the sheet bend is to extend a heaving line.

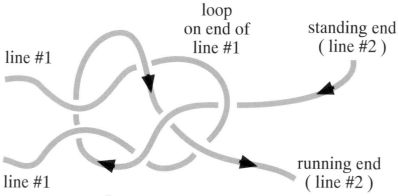

Figure 127. Sheet bend illustration

Figure 128. Sheet bend photo

1st Mate Review

1. Thimbles, shackles, clevis pins, cotter pins, grommets, pintles, gudgeons, turnbuckles, chainplates, blocks, and cleats were discussed in the 1st Mate Tools section. Can you name other boat hardware items not discussed? (Hint: look at a sailboat for other hardware items)

2. Boat paints are important for keeping the boat hull from weathering, for preventing barnacle growth on the boat bottom, for reducing friction between the hull and the water, and for making the boat look aesthetically pleasing. What were the two general classes of paints we discussed?

3. We discussed four types of line commonly used in sailing: manila, nylon, dacron, and polypropylene. List one possible correct application and one possible incorrect application for each type of line.

4. (a) In what waterway bottom condition might neither a Danforth nor a mushroom anchor work well? (b) List good qualities for both anchor types.

5. Sailors sail by the apparent wind because the apparent wind is the wind the sails "feel". How does a sailor know from where the true wind blows and how can this sailor estimate the apparent wind?

6. When sailing wing & wing, the sailor at the helm must have a good feel for the wind to avoid which special type of jibe?

7. Light wind conditions can be tricky, so experienced sailors know that sheeting out the mainsail and heeling will aid in getting the craft to go forward. Why does sheeting out and heeling help on a light wind day?

8. Draw a person overboard situation. Indicate important ideas discussed in 1st Mate Practical at each major stage on your diagram.

9. What group(s) could provide artificial respiration information and training to prepare us for an emergency situation.

10. The rolling hitch is used for applications similar to the clove hitch. The sheet bend is slightly different from the square knot and is used to attach two pieces of line. Can you tie each one correctly three consecutive times?

Bonus:
While under proper supervision, can you sail in a straight line for ten seconds while keeping your eyes closed? (This drill helps make sailors more aware of wind effects and improves a sailor's sense of boat balance.)

We're now another step closer to making Sailing a Breeze!

Captain Tools

* Heavy weather sailing

Heavy weather sailing can be dangerous. Heavy weather can be described as weather conditions that can overpower the craft. Heavy weather can include: excessive winds, rough water, driving precipitation, electrical storm activity, or a combination of all four.

Figure 129. Heavy weather sailing

When sailing in heavy winds, we should first take the standard precautions of moving weight to the windward side and keeping an eye on approaching cat's-paws. The next step one can take is to ease the sails (allowing the sails to luff slightly) to reduce wind pressure on the sails. If the luffing slows the boat to the extent rudder control is lost, one should, instead, lower the mainsail by one-third to one-half its normal height and reef the clew corner. If the winds grow too strong for the reefed mainsail technique, experienced sailors lower the mainsail completely and sail downwind to safety using only the jib.

There are times when heavy weather can be so strong that more drastic action than continued sailing with partial sails is warranted. For instance, if caught in an unforeseen storm (making reaching a safe harbor or shore risky), we should simply drop the sails and anchor while waiting for the storm to pass. And, if the boat will be overtaken by a rapidly approaching electrical storm, we should highly consider stopping the craft, lowering the sails, and removing the mast because masts attract lightening. The potential damage to or loss of equipment is inconsequential compared to the potential harm to the sailors. Keep in mind that if electrical storm activity surrounds the boat before preparatory action can be taken, the sailors should stay clear of electrically conductive standing rigging hardware and move onto a dry, non-electrically conductive surface.

We recommend being safety-minded sailors by talking to sailors experienced at sailing in the local area, learning about the local weather patterns, and listening to the up-to-the-minute weather forecast *before* deciding to sail.

Here are some **severe weather condition tips** we should all know in the event we get caught in severe weather:
- Remain calm.
- Ensure that PFD's are on properly.
- Put weight on the windward side of the boat.
- Ease the mainsheet, allowing the mainsail to luff.
- Lower the mainsail by 1/3 to 1/2 and reef its unused clew corner area to reduce sail area.
- Flatten the jib to backwind the mainsail. Backwinding the mainsail flattens its luff, which, consequently, reduces the mainsail's power.
- Keep a watchful eye on the windward side water for approaching cat's-paws.
- If on a close reach, lower the jib.
- If on a beam reach, broad reach, or run, sail by the jib alone.
- The safest points of sail are those going with the wind.
- Partly raise the centerboard to reduce the potential for being thrown broad side.
- Lower the sails and anchor the boat.
- If caught in an electrical storm, take down tall, lightning-attracting poles.
- If caught in an electrical storm and unable to take down tall, lightning-attracting poles, stay away from all standing rigging and metal surfaces.
- Use audible and visual signals to alert potential help.
- *Stay with the craft* except in the case of an extreme emergency.

Captain Theory

- Lee helm & weather helm
- Center of gravity & center of buoyancy
- Center of effort & center of lateral resistance

A boat is said to have a **weather helm** if the tiller must constantly point to windward (*weather* side) in order to maintain a straight sailing course. A boat is said to have a **lee helm** if the tiller must constantly point to leeward (*lee* side) in order to maintain a straight sailing course.

A sailboat having a weather helm turns into the wind when struck by a sudden wind gust; turning into the wind reduces pressure on the sails, turns the boat into irons, and reduces the likelihood of capsizing.

Figure 130. Weather helm

A sailboat having a lee helm turns away from the wind when struck by a sudden wind gust; turning away from the wind when on a close reach will increase pressure on the sails, which increases the likelihood of capsizing. A lee helm also puts the captain in an awkward position - leaning back to control heeling but reaching to point the tiller to leeward to maintain a straight sailing course.

Figure 131. Lee helm

Certain factors determine the type of helm the sailboat will exhibit, such as: weight distribution, sail position, sail shape, hull shape, centerboard position, and wind speed. Our objective in understanding weather and lee helms is to know how to trim the sails and hull so the boat can be sailed in the most streamlined position - *with the rudder straight.*

To understand how to correct for either a weather or lee helm, we need to understand the forces that act on a sailboat, namely gravity, buoyancy, wind (effort), and lateral resistance. To simplify the discussion, we will need to learn some definitions: center of gravity, center of buoyancy, center of effort, and center of lateral resistance.

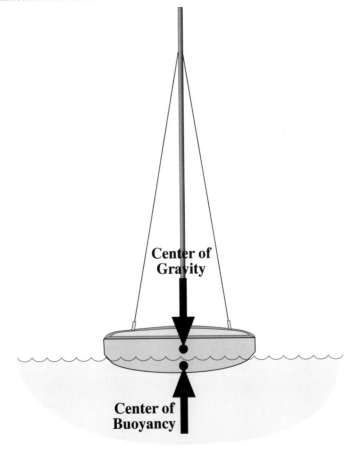

Figure 132. Center of Gravity & Center of Buoyancy

Center of Gravity: the imaginary central point representing the position where the entire weight of the boat, gear, and crew could be centered while still having the same effect on the boat. This point can move from bow to stern, port to starboard, and hull bottom to mast top.

Center of Buoyancy: the imaginary central point representing the position where the entire amount of force supporting the boat on the water could be centered while still having the same effect on the boat. This point can move along a sailboat's three axes and will vary depending on the shape of the hull beneath the water.

Gary and Mark's weight equivalence can be used to illustrate. If they sit on the port side, the center of gravity is on the port side and the center of buoyancy is centered on the part of the hull in the water. If they sit on opposite sides, the center of gravity is between them and the center of buoyancy travels back to the center of the hull. *The craft is more stable and more controllable when the centers of gravity and buoyancy are aligned at the center of the boat.* Understanding the center of gravity and the center of buoyancy aids in developing a sense of boat balance and distributing gear and crew weight on the craft.

Figure 133. COB & COG uncentered *Figure 134. COB & COG centered*

81

Center of Effort: the imaginary central point representing the position where the total wind pressure spread across the sails could be centered while still having the same effect on the boat. This position can move between the bow and stern and between the sail foot and the sail head.

Center of Lateral Resistance: the imaginary central point representing the position where all the forces that prevent side-slipping could be centered while still having the same effect on the boat. This position can move between the bow and stern and between the bottom of the centerboard and the water's surface on the leeward side.

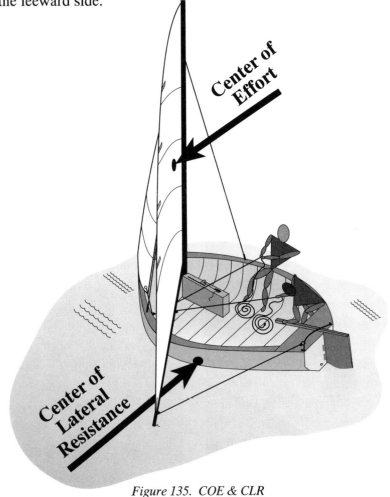

Figure 135. COE & CLR

If we draw imaginary vertical lines through the center of effort and center of lateral resistance, we can better picture how these forces physically act on the sailboat to help create either a weather or lee helm.

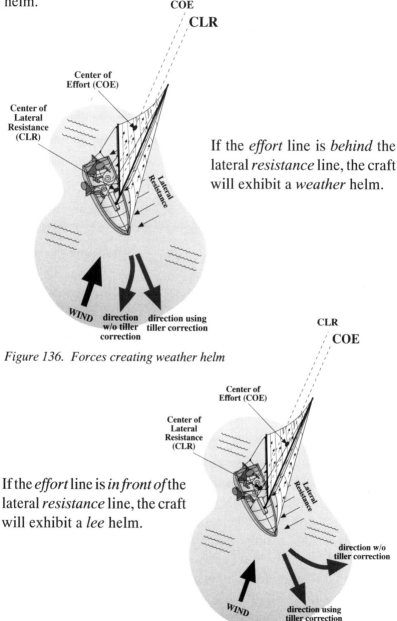

If the *effort* line is *behind* the lateral *resistance* line, the craft will exhibit a *weather* helm.

Figure 136. Forces creating weather helm

If the *effort* line is *in front of* the lateral *resistance* line, the craft will exhibit a *lee* helm.

Figure 137. Forces creating lee helm

The weathervane provides a good analogy to help us understand the results forces that help create weather and lee helms. Pretend the pedestal is the center of all water forces on the hull and the fingertip is the center of all wind forces on the sails.

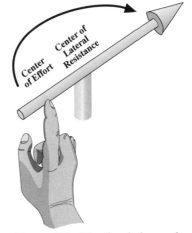

If the finger pushes on the weathervane *behind* the pedestal, the weathervane turns to face the wind, which is a weather helm effect.

Figure 138. Weather helm analogy

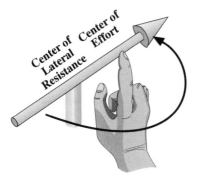

Figure 139. Lee helm analogy

If the finger pushes on the weathervane *in front* of the pedestal, the weathervane turns to face away from the wind, which is a lee helm effect.

If the sailboat has a weather helm and no attempt is made to keep the boat on its sailing course, the sailboat will stop turning after it has turned fully into the wind (i.e., irons). We should now understand that we can simply shift our weight toward stern to reduce the weather helm because the center of lateral resistance will shift toward stern to balance against the center of effort. In the weathervane analogy, the finger would be pushing on the weathervane directly over the pedestal when the COE is together with the CLR; therefore, the weathervane will not rotate, and, likewise, neither will the boat. In the case of a lee helm, weight should be shifted slowly toward bow until the boat can stay on a straight sailing course without having to point the tiller to leeward.

To complete our basic theoretical understanding of sailboat dynamics, we, as Captains, should understand how the four basic forces combine and should know what adjustments can be made to keep the craft moving at peak efficiency. The best example for putting it all together is the case in which our sailboat is struck by a sudden wind gust while sailing on a close reach. The first obvious effect is that the boat will heel. The heeling is caused by the height of the sail force (COE) over the boat's center of rotation (COR), located approximately in the center of the hull above the COB. The wind will have less ability to make the boat heel when the distance between the COE and the COR is short. This means that when we slightly lower the mainsail and reef the clew corner, we not only reduce the mainsail area but also shorten the distance between the COE and the boat's COR - both of which reduce capsizing potential.

Next, when the sailboat heels, the COB shifts approximately to the center of the hull still in the water. Our immediate reaction is to shift weight to windward. This is good because shifting weight to windward moves the COG to windward. As we have discussed, moving the COG to the side of the boat without raised sails makes the boat heel toward the COG. In the case of heeling to leeward due to wind force on the sails, we want to use our weight to counteract the wind gust making the boat heel to leeward. Often, sailboats are equipped with hiking straps or a trapeze that allows sailors to get the COG well out to windward, allowing the sails to take on a great amount of wind without causing the boat to excessively heel. If the heeling force caused by moving crew weight to windward equals that of the heeling force caused by the wind, the boat will stop heeling. If the heeling force caused

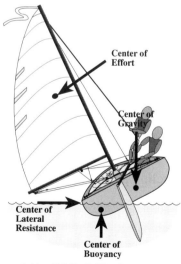

Figure 140. COG, COB, COE, & CLR

by moving weight to windward is less than that of the wind's heeling force, the boat may continue to heel until capsizing occurs. As we have discussed, sheeting out the sails or heading up toward or into irons will reduce wind pressure on the sails, which, of course, reduces the heeling angle.

Assuming we have controlled the excessive heeling, have trimmed the sails and hull, and are still travelling across the water in the midst of our hypothetical, prolonged, wind gust, we will fine tune the CLR to remove a lee or weather helm created by the changing wind

Figure 141. Heeling corrected

and weight on the boat. We will most often find the craft has developed a weather helm that is caused by the movement of the CLR toward the bow because of the increased bow wave (water being pushed by the bow traveling into it). Note that the density of lateral resistance forces is increased at the bow, so the center of all lateral resistance forces moves forward. When the CLR moves in front of the sail's COE, we have learned that we must point the tiller to windward in order to maintain a straight sailing course. Remembering that a tiller not pointing directly toward the bow is inefficient because of its drag (like sailing with a bent centerboard), we can simply shift our body weight toward the stern to shift the CLR back along the keel-line until it is equal with the COE. This removes the weather helm and allows sailing with the tiller pointed straight toward bow to resume. In effect, we have corrected a weather helm by adding some lee helm. Sailors often prefer a boat that turns into rather than away from the wind during a wind gust because it is less prone to capsizing since the sail area exposed to the gust will get smaller, thereby reducing the gust's heeling ability to make the boat heel or capsize.

Our goal in understanding the forces that act on a sailboat is to be able to use these forces both to keep the boat upright and to maximize our sailing efficiency. With practice, we will be able to handle the wind gust scenario as if it were second nature.

Captain Practical

- Solo sailing
- Beaching

Solo sailing can be exciting. Let's look at some additional responsibilities placed on the captain's shoulders when no crew is available. Jib control is one such responsibility. Either the captain holds the jib and mainsheets, which can be difficult in windy situations, or the jib sheet can be cleated. Because constant sail trimming cannot occur when the jib sheet is cleated, sailing performance is sacrificed. Remember that we change the jib control to the leeward jib sheet only after fully coming about in order to help the sailboat cross through irons. This works out well for the solo sailor because changing the jib sheet is an easier task when sailing on a tack rather than during changing tacks. Because jib control is not necessary in the single sail rig, the

Figure 142. Solo sailing

solo sailor can concentrate on other solo sailing issues, such as correcting for a lee helm and correcting for sideslipping tendency. When solo sailing, a tiller equipped with a tiller extender allows the solo sailor to move his or her weight toward the bow. We recall that having too much weight far back in the stern can cause a lee helm because the center of lateral resistance (being a function of the center of gravity) is aft of the center of effort and, in some craft, because a light bow can allow the bow to be pushed to leeward by strong winds. Solo sailing with and without a tiller extender will help us better understand the usefulness of having a tiller extender and emphasize what the proper use of it can do for us in terms of sailing the boat more efficiently.

When solo sailing, sitting on leeward may be necessary to prevent sideslipping, especially when sailing a craft with a flat bottom hull in light wind conditions. But, because a captain moves the tiller in reference to the windward and leeward (not in reference to the captain's position), sailing from leeward is no problem.

Beaching is made more difficult when solo sailing because centerboard or daggerboard control responsibility is added to the solo sailor's tasks of controlling the sails, tiller, and lateral resistance. When beaching:

- Be prepared to raise the centerboard or daggerboard.
- Ensure the rudder will raise before reaching shallow water.
- Attempt to approach the destination on a run or expect to increase the lateral resistance by sitting toward or on the leeward side. Keep in mind that because the centerboard or daggerboard must be raised, the boat will experience a reduction in lateral resistance.
- Avoid running the craft onto the sand - head up into irons and allow the sails to luff.
- Do not attempt to exit the craft before it has come to a complete stop and safe deboarding is possible.

Figure 143. Preparing to beach the craft

Captain Knots

- Eye splice
- Whipping
- Making a mooring
- Monkey's fist

Up to this point we've learned knots which are used while sailing. The next two additions to our marlinspike seamanship, splicing and whipping, are useful in making anchor lines, mooring lines, and dock lines.

To prepare for **splicing**, we first take three pieces of tape, each approximately one loop's worth around the line, and set aside. Next, take the three braid line - 3/8" nylon is easy to use while learning - and tape in the direction of the rope twist approximately 3" to 6" above the braiding end. This piece of tape will prevent the line from completely unraveling.

Figure 144. Unbraid and tape

Now separate the piece of line into its three component strands and tape the three loose ends tightly using the three pieces of tape set aside earlier. Leave a small piece of line showing beyond those pieces of tape so the tape does not slide off the end.

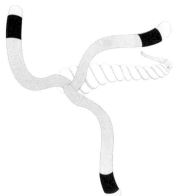

Figure 145. Unbraid and tape

We are now ready to make the **eye splice**. Start with the standing end away from you. Next, take the running end, point it away from you, and lay it on top of the standing end. *Your permanent loop size is determined by the loop created by the length of running end folded back onto the standing end.* At this point, two of the three component running end strands should be draping over opposite sides of the standing end, with the third lying on top of the standing end. Slightly back-twist the standing end to open a gap between the three component strands.

Next, take the running end center strand and weave it into the standing end by guiding it through the gap beneath the top standing end strand (which we raised and separated by back-twisting the standing end). Back-twist the standing end and guide the left running end strand through the gap just left of where the center strand came out. Take the right running strand and weave it under the standing end strand not yet on top of a running end strand. Each running end strand should now be 120° apart. Braid

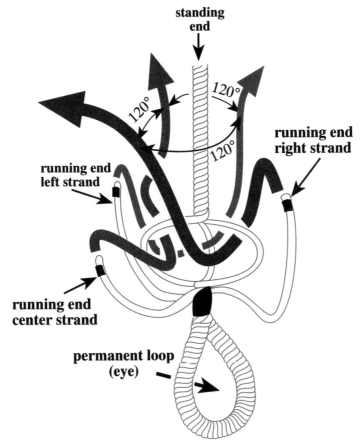

Figure 146. Eye splice, 1st weave illustration

over and under in a clockwise fashion (against the natural twist of the standing end line) until a little more than the tape on the running end component strands is showing. Rolling the completed splice between our hands will make the braid smooth.

Figure 147. Completed eyesplice

To secure the end of the splice, we can use whipping line. **Whipping line** is thin and often wax-coated. Let's learn one **whipping** technique. Make a loop on top of the three-braid line with the whipping line. Twist the whipping line running end around the three-braid line, working up the whipping line loop. Put the running end through the loop. Pull the standing end so the loop is beneath the twist. Tie a square knot with the excess running and standing ends of the whipping line. Turn the running and standing ends in opposite directions around the line being whipped, and complete the whip by tying another square knot.

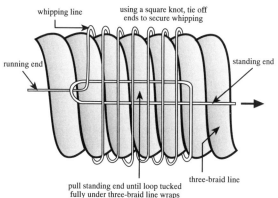

Figure 148. Whipping illustration

Let's now look at how a **mooring** is made. Keep in mind that no line should rub against metal. Starting at the anchor, connect the chain to it through the use of a shackle. Connect the other end of the chain to the thimble (eye-spliced in the line), using another shackle. A chain weighing as much as or more than the anchor should be attached between the anchor and line to buffer boat movement from dragging or even picking up the anchor. Connect the buoy to a second thimble, eye-spliced in the line, with a shackle. 1/2" nylon line is standard for most anchor lines. 1/2" line is thick for small boats, but easy to handle. Generally, the anchor line length should be five to ten times the depth of water in which it is used. Connect the clip to a small line. Connect the clip line to the buoy - use a thimble and shackle to make this connection. Be sure that enough clip line is used. The buoy should be upright at all times. Avoid connecting line to moving metal parts. Use stainless steel, nylon coated, or galvanized metal parts to protect chains, anchors, thimbles, shackles, and other metal parts exposed to water from rusting.

Figure 149. Mooring with mushroom anchor

A **monkey's fist knot** is useful for heaving lines and is fun to make. Inside the monkey's fist is a block of wood which floats.

Figure 150. Monkey's Fist photo

Figure 151. Mark with decorative monkey's fist

When tossing a heaving line with a monkey's fist or other such flotation attached to the heaving line's tossing end, the crew member tossing the line should attempt to place the flotation beyond - rather than short of or at - the receiver. This tossing technique will avoid injury and enable the crew to pull the flotation to the receiver instead of requiring a time consuming re-toss by the crew should the toss be too short.

Captain Review

1. Heavy weather sailing must be accompanied by heavy weather sailing precautions to ensure sailor safety. (a) List three or more preventative measures against capsizing which an experienced sailor might use and, (b) list three common sense safety measures to be ready for a worst-case scenario.

2. A sailboat which exhibits the characteristic of floating flat on the surface of the water while at rest is said to have its center of _____ directly over its center of _____ in the center of the craft.

3. A sailboat that has either a weather or lee helm does not sail at its most optimum speed because its tiller must be pointed to windward or leeward, respectively, in order to maintain a straight course. A tiller that does not point directly to the bow results in a rudder that creates some drag. List some physical boat attributes which contribute to causing one type of helm or the other.

4. By positioning ourselves and/or crew member(s) correctly about the craft, we can offset the craft's helm tendency. (a) Assuming the sails are well trimmed, in which direction (fore or aft) would a sailor well in tune with his or her craft move to offset a weather helm? (b) A lee helm?

5. Sometimes compensating for a weather or lee helm results in "plowing" the water - too much bow or stern hull displacement. This "plowing" is a result of adjusting weight to align the center of effort and center of lateral resistance to reduce the weather or lee helm. Rather than only using a weight shift, what other methods might an experienced sailor use to aid in reducing a weather or lee helm?

Congratulations on your efforts...

Figure 152. Your instructors congratulate you!

6. A sailboat may have its sail set so high that the craft tends to heel quite easily. What role does the center of effort play and how might we make the sailboat less likely to capsize in the case presented above?

7. Solo sailing challenges and rewards the sailor. (a) List a solo sailor's added responsibilities due to having no crew. (b) Why is a tiller extender important for the solo sailor in terms of correcting a weather or lee helm?

8. When beaching a sailboat, we need to raise the centerboard or daggerboard and rudder as we approach the shore. We know from the seed theory that our craft will tend to sideslip when reducing lateral resistance. What advice would be good to give others to help them reduce sideslipping as they approach shore?

9. Use a piece of 3/8" three-braid nylon line and some tape to weave an eyesplice. Having a marlinspike on hand is useful to help work the line. Complete the eyesplice by using whipping line to secure the splice.

10. Why are thimbles spliced into mooring lines where connections between the mooring line and shackles, chains, and other metal hardware are made?

Bonus:
Teach others the sport of sailing to re-enforce the knowledge you have gained through these lessons.

...and thank you for helping us to make Sailing a Breeze for you!

Figure 153. And we'll all sail happily ever after...

Index of Figures

Index of Figures

Index of Figures

Index

Crew Answers

1. **PFD's.** (a) Type II PFDs provide buoyancy and keeps breathing passages clear of water. Type III PFDs provide buoyancy and more movement freedom than Type II PFDs. (b) Unexpected situations could be a boating accident or a person overboard. (see pages 10-12)
2. **Safety equipment.** (a) Extra Line - towing a canoe to safety. Whistle - alerting others of a need for assistance. First aid kit - bandaging a wound or scrape. (b) Two-way communication device - reaching help when no help is within the immediate area. Wool blanket - sudden cold weather. (see pages 14-15)
3. **Sailboat nomenclature.** bow, starboard, port, stern, gunwale, main stay, centerboard cabin, centerboard, shrouds, turnbuckle or chainplate, mast, boom, deck, transom, tiller, rudder, traveler. (see pages 16-17)
4. **Boarding.** When boarding any craft, we place one hand on the boat we are boarding and place the other hand on the boat or dock from which we are deboarding. We then "shift our weight" behind our hands from boat to boat or dock to boat so the boat being entered does not slide away from us, potentially landing us in the drink (or worse). (see pages 18-19)
5. **Rigging.** We recommend raising the jib after the mainsail for two reasons. The first reason is so that the jib clew (and the jib sheet clip) is not snapping wildly about the head and eyes. The second reason is that a jib filled with wind will turn a floating boat sideways to the wind (out of irons). When this happens, the boat will begin to move forward and, when attached to a dock or mooring by the bow, the boat may capsize. (see pages 19-22)
6. **Reading the wind.** (a) Three ways to determine wind direction are: looking at the direction the ripples and cat's-paws on the water are traveling, feeling the wind cool our skin when the boat is stationary, and facing the wind until hearing it equally in both ears. When feeling or listening to the wind, one should be on the windward side of the craft so as not to incorrectly sense wind redirected by the sails. (b) We describe wind to others by indicating the direction from where the wind is coming and pointing in that direction. (see pages 23-24)
7. **Controlling the helm.** During normal sailing conditions, the captain sits on the <u>windward</u> side of the craft and keeps his or her attention <u>forward</u>. The captain's bow-side hand controls the <u>mainsheet</u> and stern-side hand controls the <u>tiller</u>. (see page 25)
8. **Excessive heeling.** If the weight of the captain (helmsperson) and crew are not enough to adequately control excessive heeling, the captain could let out the mainsail to *reduce* wind pressure on the sail or point the tiller to the side opposite the wind (leeward) to turn the sailboat into the wind (irons) to *remove* wind pressure from the sail. (see pages 25-26)
9. **Rule of the Road.** The basic rule of the road is avoid collisions. (see page 27)
10. **Rigging knots.** Lines tied off with a cleat hitch are the halyards, outhaul, and downhaul. Lines tied off with a figure 8 knot are the main and jib sheets. The first three lines are used in sailboat set up; the last two lines are used during sailboat operation. (see pages 28-29)

2nd Mate Answers

1. **Rigging.** Some standing rigging parts are the shrouds and mainstay. Some running rigging parts are the halyards and sheets. (see pages 32-33)
2. **Sail nomenclature.** (a) Parts of the mainsail are the head, luff, tack, foot, clew, leech, and battens. (b) Phrases: "The *head* is at the top of the sail", "the sail stands on its *foot*", "the sail is *tack*-ed to where the boom and mast meet", "the *clew* has no clew, otherwise it would be closer to the mast", "the *leech* is leeching onto the rest of the sail." (see page 34)
3. **Sail care.** (a) One method of reefing a mainsail is: lowering, folding, rolling, laying and tying the mainsail securely to the boom. (b) We may wish to store the sail in a cool, dry place rather than reefing it if the sail is wet or wet weather is predicted. Always hang and dry a wet sail because a wet, rolled sail will mildew, causing discoloration and damage to the sail. (see pages 35-36)
4. **Slot effect.** The low pressure area develops behind a sail when sailing because the wind passing behind the sail displaces air molecules, creating a virtual vacuum or low pressure area. (see pages 37-38)
5. **Seed theory.** (a) The seed theory suggests that the wind on the sailboat's windward side and the water on the sailboat's leeward side is analogous to "fingers" that squeeze and shoot forward a watermelon seed. (b) The boat gets shot forward because the bow makes it easy for the craft to move in that direction, as opposed to the flat stern. (see page 37-39)
6. (a) Sail only downwind (to shore or safety); (b) create a boat heel, using body weight, to add lateral resistance; (3) sheet out the mainsail farther than optimal trim to help pull the sailboat forward instead of off at an angle. (see page 39)
7. **Points-of-sail.** (a) Irons, beat, close reach, beam reach, broad reach, run. (b) On a port tack, the wind strikes *port* first. (see page 40-41)
8. **Trimming sails and hull.** (a) To trim a sail, we slowly sheet it out until it begins to luff, then sheet it in until the sail is smooth. Sail trimming is done to use the wind efficiently. To trim the hull, one adjusts body weight about the boat. Hull trimming is done to balance the boat and to provide lateral resistance. (b) Sail and hull trimming occur *continuously*. (see page 42)
9. **Changing tacks.** (a) When coming about, the bow is said to cross through irons. (b) When jibing, the stern is said to cross through irons. (see pages 43-46).
10. **Irons.** An experienced sailor gets out of irons by backwinding the jib to turn the bow. On a single sail craft, pulling the boom to windward usually turns the craft out of irons. (see pages 47-48).
11. **Capsizing.** (a) Capsize procedure: 1. save yourself, 2. count heads, 3. swim the boat into irons, 4. upright the boat by putting weight on the centerboard or daggerboard, 5. re-enter the craft, 6. check physical conditions. Also one may find it necessary to lower (but not detach) the sails because of the weight of water on them. And, flotation may be important to place on the end of the mast to prevent the craft from turtling. (b) Irons keeps a righted boat stationary. (c) A capsized boat is easier to spot than a lone swimmer. (see pages 50-51)
12. The coast guard and local Red Cross chapter. (see page 53)

1st Mate Answers

1. **Sailboat hardware.** Shroud wire, spinnaker poles, screws, boat bumpers, shroud spreaders, eyehooks, jib snaps, boom vang, eyeplates, and eyestraps are some examples of boat hardware not discussed in 1st Mate Tools. Additional items can be found in good marine stores. (see pages 58-62)
2. **Boat paints.** The two general classes of paints discussed were topside and bottomside paints. Recall that there are many subclasses of each and researching the right paints for your application is recommended. (see page 63)
3. **Boat line.** (see pages 64-65)

line material	one possible correct use	one possible improper use
manila	dock handrail	sheet line
nylon	mooring line	sheet line
dacron	sheets and halyards	waterskiing line
polypropylene	ring buoy line	sheet line

4. **Anchors.** (a) A smooth, hard, waterway bottom condition is one in which neither a Danforth nor mushroom anchor would work well. (b) A mushroom anchor likes a muddy waterway bottom condition because it works best when covered with mud to take full advantage of its shape, which creates a suction force. The Danforth anchor likes to wedge its spades beneath rocks or bury them into sand. (see page 65-66)
5. **True and apparent wind.** A sailor knows from where the true wind blows by watching the direction the cat's paws travel on the water in his or her immediate area. One way to estimate the apparent wind is to sit on the windward side, look into the wind, and hear it equally in both ears. The direction faced is from where the apparent wind blows. (see pages 67-68)
6. **Goosewing jibe.** Sailing wing & wing can often lead to a goosewing jibe. (see page 69).
7. **Light wind conditions.** (a) On a light wind condition day, sheeting out allows any hint of wind to get around the sail, and heeling will cause the sail to curve under its own weight. Heeling also adds lateral resistance that helps resist sideslipping, which is important in light wind conditions. (see page 70)
8. **Person overboard.** "keep eye on victim", "toss flotation device to victim", "stop and wait if victim can swim to boat", "use distress signals", "count to five", "come about", "jibe", "victim on windward", "check physical conditions". (see pages 70-72)
9. **Artificial respiration.** The (American) Red Cross, local hospitals, and Coast Guard are just some groups that can provide artificial respiration information and training to prepare us for an emergency situation.
10. **1st Mate knots.** (see pages 74-75)

Captain Answers

1. **Heavy weather sailing.** (a) Raising the mainsail only two-thirds and reefing the clew corner to reduce the sail area, sailing with only a mainsail, educating crew members on hull trimming techniques, sailing without battens, and choosing to wait for calmer winds are some of the preventative measures a captain can take to avoid capsizing on a heavy weather day. (b) Three common sense safety measures a captain might use to be ready for worst case scenarios are mandating the wearing of PFD's, running a controlled capsizing drill with the crew before sailing a heavy weather day, and providing for shore rescue assistance. (see pages 77-78)

2. **COG & COB.** A sailboat's center of <u>gravity</u> directly over its center of <u>buoyancy</u> in the center of the craft makes it float flat on the water's surface. (see pages 80-81)

3. **Lee and weather helms.** Some physical boat attributes that cause a weather or lee helm are its bow-to-stern weight balance, center of gravity, mast position, hull and sail shape, and centerboard position. Generally, the following cause a weather helm: center of gravity toward bow, mast position toward stern, centerboard toward bow. (see pages 79-84)

4. **Lee and weather helms.** Moving weight aft will offset a weather helm. Moving weight fore will offset a lee helm. Keep in mind that course direction and sail and hull trim must be kept constant when proving this to yourself. (see pages 84-86)

5. **Lee and weather helms.** To correct a weather helm: the mast can be tilted forward by adjusting the mainstay hardware, usually a turnbuckle or chainplate, or slightly raising the centerboard. To offset a lee helm: the mainsail can be raked back and rudder angled back. By working with fundamental means of adjusting the sailboat's centers of effort and lateral resistance, one will not need to make major weight adjustments on the craft, which can result in "plowing" the water. (see pages 85-86)

6. **COE & heeling.** To minimize heeling and capsizing potential caused by a high center of effort, an experienced captain will lower the mainsail by lowering the boom on sloop rigs with that feature, or slide up the halyard toward the mainsail head on a lateen rig. Both methods of adjustment should be made *prior* to setting sail. (see pages 85-86)

7. **Solo sailing.** (a) A solo sailor, besides having to control the mainsheet and tiller, must also control the jib (on a sloop rig), perform all windward/leeward adjustments, monitor cat's-paws, and coordinate mooring and beaching exercises. (b) A tiller extender allows the solo sailor to shift his or her weight forward to reduce a lee helm. (see pages 87-88)

8. **Beaching.** The advice experienced Captains would give to others to help them control their sideslipping when beaching a sailboat is to head to shore on a broad reach or run point-of-sail, to lower the jib, to sheet out the mainsail, to create an artificial heel to leeward, and to raise the centerboard or daggerboard as required rather than simply raising it fully. This advice applies what good captains know as maximizing the lateral resistance and moving the center of effort toward stern. (see page 88)

9. **Eyesplice.** (see pages 89-91)

10. **Moorings.** A well-made mooring will never have a bare line tied to either another line or moving metal part because wear and fatigue will soon develop at these joints. This is why thimbles are spiced into the line to form the eyes used in making these connections. One should be sure that shackle clevis pins are prevented from turning (due to constant mooring motion) by securing the clevis pin in place with wire. (see page 92)

Rob Tannenbaum
Photographer, black & white photographs

Amy L. Solomon
Photographer, cover photographs

Mark & Gary Solomon

Gary and Mark Solomon founded Aquatics Unlimited in 1989. Aquatics Unlimited is a watersport education organization which offers hands-on training in rowing, canoeing, kayaking, waterskiing, windsurfing, and sailing. Both Gary and Mark earned four instructorships and ten other certifications through the American Red Cross. After many years of teaching children from the ages eight through fifteen, Gary and Mark began Aquatics Unlimited to train American Camping Association affiliated camp waterfront staffs and have been involved with adult education programs.

Product Information

"Sailing's a Breeze!" and *"Paddle to Perfection!"* are part of the Aquatics Unlimited *"Getting off the Ground!"* instructional watersport series. Both instructional boating courses are available in book, video, and water-safe quick reference guide formats. The videos are professionally produced, and the author-illustrated, photo-packed books provide students with questions and answers to measure learning progress. Great for beginners, intermediates, and those teaching others. SAB! and PTP! are book and video shelf musts!

Sailing's a Breeze!

Paddle to Perfection!

Crew

- ☐ safety
- ☐ safety equipment
- ☐ use of PFD
- ☐ nomenclature
- ☐ boarding & deboarding
- ☐ rigging & derigging
- ☐ securing the craft
- ☐ reading the wind
- ☐ sailing the boat
- ☐ excessive heeling
- ☐ basic rule of the road
- ☐ cleat hitch
- ☐ figure 8 knot

2nd Mate

- ☐ sailboat rigging
- ☐ sail nomenclature
- ☐ care of sails
- ☐ reefing the sails
- ☐ seed theory
- ☐ slot effect
- ☐ points of sail
- ☐ coming about & jibing
- ☐ getting out of irons
- ☐ getting underway
- ☐ capsizing
- ☐ trimming sails & hull
- ☐ rules of the road
- ☐ clove hitch
- ☐ bowline
- ☐ square knot

1st Mate

- ☐ sailboat hardware
- ☐ protect & repair mat'l
- ☐ types of line
- ☐ anchor types
- ☐ true & apparent wind
- ☐ wing & wing
- ☐ light wind conditions
- ☐ person overboard
- ☐ artificial respiration
- ☐ rolling hitch
- ☐ sheet bend

Captain

- ☐ heavy weather sailing
- ☐ weather helm
- ☐ lee helm
- ☐ center of gravity
- ☐ center of buoyancy
- ☐ center of effort
- ☐ center of lateral resistance
- ☐ solo sailing
- ☐ beaching
- ☐ eye splice
- ☐ whipping
- ☐ making a mooring
- ☐ monkey's fist

112

Aquatics Unlimited, Inc.
8 Park Plaza #208
Boston, MA 02116

Complete this registration card and receive a *free official* "*Sailing's a Breeze!*" Certificate of Completion!

Yes! I am extremely pleased with the "*Sailing's a Breeze!*" instructional sailing product and would like to order additional copies for family and friends.

☐ Video, _____ copies @ $24.95 ea.
☐ Book, _____ copies @ $14.95 ea.
☐ Toolbox, _____ copies @ $11.95 ea.
  and / or
☐ _____ complete sets @ $39.95 ea.

Please add $5.00 for shipping & handling.
MA residents include a 5% sales tax.

Aquatics Unlimited
8 Park Plaza #208
Boston, MA 02116
(617) 551-8200

---

1. Name: _____
   Address: _____
   City: _____ State: _____ Zip: _____
2. Age: _____
3. How long have you been sailing?
   ☐ fewer than 2 years   ☐ 5 - 10 years
   ☐ 2 - 5 years   ☐ greater than 10 years
4. Do you belong to a sailing club or team? ☐ Yes ☐ No
5. How many times a year do you sail?
   ☐ 10 or fewer ☐ 10 - 25 ☐ more than 25
6. Do you own a sailboat? ☐ Yes ☐ No
7. Where do you typically sail? ☐ lake ☐ bay ☐ ocean
8. What size boat do you regularly sail?
   ☐ 12' or fewer ☐ 18' or fewer ☐ larger than 18'
9. How did you attain "*Sailing's a Breeze!*"?
   ☐ retail store   ☐ sailing course
   ☐ marine (boating) store ☐ gift
   ☐ Aquatics Unlimited   ☐ other
10. How would you rate this product as a learning tool?
    poor 1 2 3 4 5 excellent
11. Would you recommend this product to a:
    ☐ beginner sailor ☐ intermediate sailor ☐ advanced sailor
12. Would you be interested in a similar product to learn:
    ☐ windsurfing ☐ canoeing ☐ rowing
    ☐ waterskiing ☐ kayaking ☐ knots & splices